ARCHITECTURE
&ORNAMENT

The Diagram Group

Editor	Randal Gray
Editorial assistant	James Dallas
Art director	Darren Bennett
Artists	Peter Crossman, Brian Hewson, Lee Lawrence, Paul McCauley, Philip Patenall, Micky Pledge, Tim Scrivens
Consultant	Robert Tavernor PhD, RIBA

STUDIO VISTA
an imprint of
Cassell
Villiers House, 41/47 Strand
London WC2N 5JE

First published 1990

British Library Cataloguing in Publication Data
White, Antony
  Architecture and ornament: a visual guide. (Visual guides to the decorative arts.)
  1. Buildings. Architectural features
  I. Title   II. Robertson, Bruce *1934–*   III. Series
  720

ISBN 0-289-80035-8

Printed in Portugal by Resopal Indústria Gráfica, Ida. – Sintra

ARCHITECTURE & ORNAMENT

A·VISUAL·GUIDE

ANTONY WHITE · BRUCE ROBERTSON

STUDIO
VISTA

Preface

ARCHITECTURE AND ORNAMENT is the first of a series of visual guides which have been designed as ingenious reference books for the student and enthusiast—as books to be used as field guides to identify objects as seen, or to illustrate a term known but not visually understood.

ARCHITECTURE AND ORNAMENT provides the reader with a guide both to the appearance and the naming of the most common and interesting architectural parts and decorative motifs used in Western architecture from Classical times to the Modern Age.

The reader can start either from the glossary text or the plates —either by looking up a term or naming the headword which will then cross refer to the illustrations; or by using the plates of illustrations to identify a term and hence its place in the alphabetical text.

The illustration plates, which are divided into types of buildings, structures, and ornament, provide line drawings of the major structural and decorative parts of Western buildings. They include civil, military and church architecture, decorative motifs, emblems and heraldic devices.

The main text or glossary of terms consists of 1500 entries made up of short descriptions, and references to the illustrations, of types of building and their structure, varieties of ornament, and technical terms. The glossary text includes 160 thumbnail sketches of all the major styles of Western architecture and famous architects—illustrated in the margins by over 100 concise line drawings of typical and eminent examples of their output.

The chronology of Western ARCHITECTURE AND ORNAMENT is clarified by the provision of a timechart showing all the major styles. This timechart not only illustrates the duration of the great styles, but also demonstrates how they spread to ten different countries and regions at different times and in different sequences. To complement these period chronologies, there are also maps showing the major architectural sites of the Classical, Romanesque, Gothic and Renaissance styles.

Contents

PLATE LIST

SECTION 1: **BUILDINGS**

1.01 Classical house and temple: layout	**1.07** Medieval castle and fortress bastion
1.02 Classical baths and theatre: layout	**1.08** Church exterior parts
	1.09 Church interior layout
1.03 Classical facade, columniation and layout	**1.10** Church furnishing
	1.11 Church windows
1.04 Classical orders: columns	**1.12** Church wall parts
1.05 Classical orders: column parts	**1.13** Medieval house
	1.14 Terrace house
1.06 Ancient and medieval columns and capitals	**1.15** Modern house

SECTION 2: **STRUCTURES**

2.01 Walls: stone	**2.10** Wood structures
2.02 Brickwork 1	**2.11** Staircases
2.03 Brickwork 2	**2.12** Arch parts
2.04 Walls: wood	**2.13** Arch types
2.05 Roof types	**2.14** Window parts
2.06 Domes	**2.15** Window types
2.07 Vaults	**2.16** Door parts
2.08 Roofing	**2.17** Door types
2.09 Roof supports	

SECTION 3: **ORNAMENT**

3.01 Mouldings 1	**3.06** Devices 2
3.02 Mouldings 2	**3.07** Heraldic devices 1
3.03 Motifs 1	**3.08** Heraldic devices 2
3.04 Motifs 2	**3.09** Heraldic devices 3
3.05 Devices 1	**3.10** Drawing projections

1.01

A **Roman town house**
1 Vestibule
2 Fauces
3 Cellae
4 Cubicula
5 Atrium
6 Impluvium
7 Ala
8 Tablinum
9 Apotheca
10 Androne
11 Triclinium
12 Peristyle and hortus
13 Cubicula
14 Exedra
15 Oecus
16 Latrina
17 Culina

B **Greek temple**
18 Opisthodomos
19 Parthenon/Adyton/
Sanctuary
20 Cult statue
21 Naos/Cella
22 Pronaos
23 Crepidoma
24 Peristyle
25 Acroterion

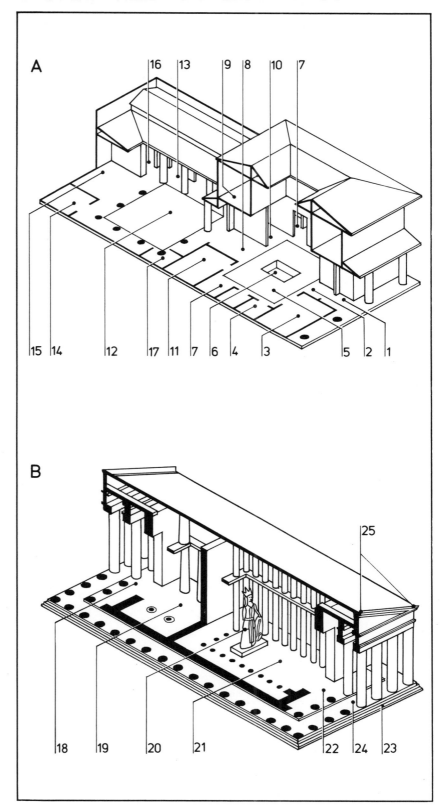

A **Public Baths (Thermae)**
(a) **Central building**
1 Frigidarium
2 Vestibule
3 Apodyterium
4 Central hall
5 Ephebeum
6 Suites of bathrooms
7 Tepidarium
8 Calidarium (caldarium)
(b) **Surrounding complex**
9 Exedra
10 Principal entrance
11 Quiet rooms
12 Library
13 Theatre

B **Theatre**
14 Diazoma
15 Cuneus
16 Parodos
17 Logeion
18 Scene building (scaena/scena)
19 Auditorium
20 Hyposkenion
21 Proscenion (proskenion)

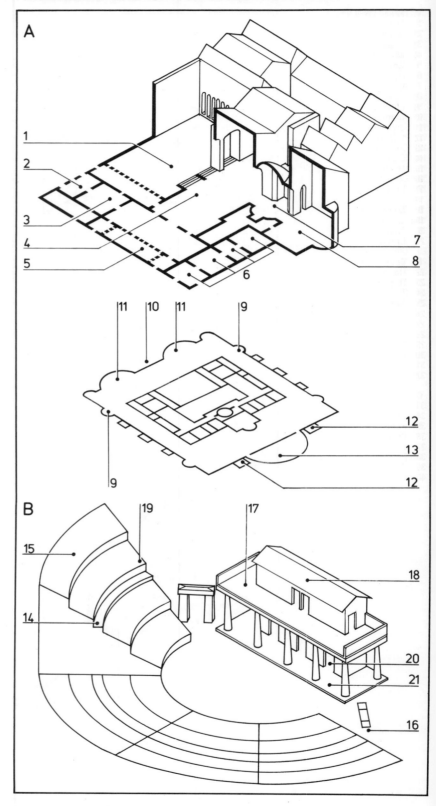

©DIAGRAM

A **Facade features**
1 Tympanum
2 Acroterion
3 Triglyph
4 Metope
5 Tenia
6 Regula
7 Guttae
8 Abacus
9 Echinus
10 Annulet
11 Stylobate
12 Quadriga
13 Pediment
14 Cornice
15 Frieze
16 Architrave
17 Entablature
18 Capital
19 Shaft
19a Entasis
20 Column
21 Crepidoma

B **Columniation**
22 Henostyle
23 Distyle
24 Tristyle
25 Tetrastyle
26 Penastyle
27 Hexastyle
28 Heptastyle
29 Octastyle
30 Enneastyle
31 Decastyle
32 Dodecastyle

C **Layout**
33 Distyle in Antis
34 Amphi-prostyle
35 Peripteral
36 Pseudo-peripteral
37 Dipteral
38 Pseudo-dipteral
39 Pteroma
40 Pteron

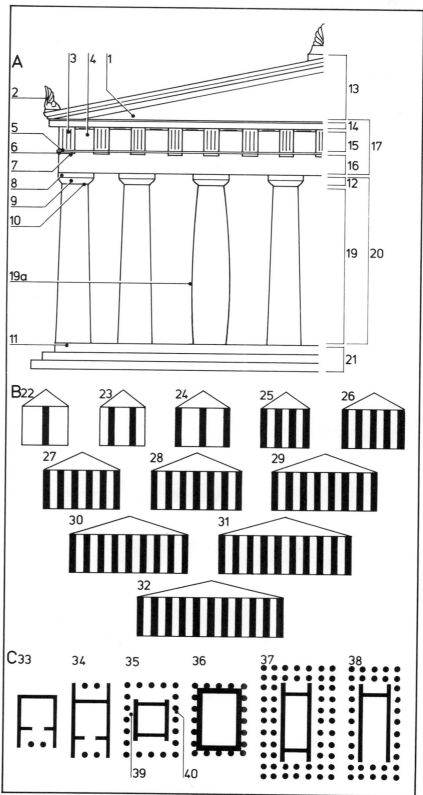

1.04

A Classical orders
1 Doric
2 Ionic
3 Corinthian

B Derived orders
4 Tuscan
5 Doric Roman
6 Composite

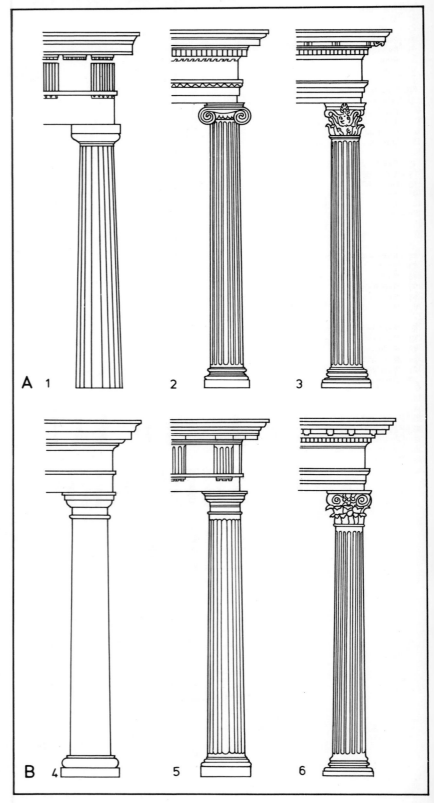

©DIAGRAM

A The Doric order
1 Mutule
2 Triglyph
3 Guttae
4 Necking (Trachelion)
4a Hypotrachelion
5 Astragal

B The Ionic order
6 Flat frieze
7 Pulvinated (convex) frieze
8 Volutes, diagonally placed

C The Corinthian order
9 Modillion
10 Dentils
11 Acanthus foliage in outline showing its arrangement round the bell

D Pedestal
12 Torus
13 Scotia
14 Plinth
15 Die/Dado
16 Base
17 Pedestal (Attic base)

E Inter-columniation
18 Pycnostyle
19 Systyle
20 Eustyle
21 Diastyle
22 Araeostyle

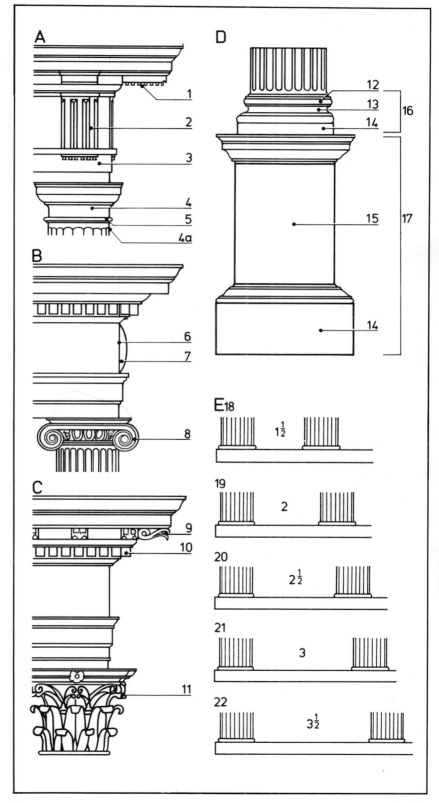

A Column parts
1 Cap (capital)
2 Abacus
3 Shaft
4 Base
5 Banding
6 Necking
7 Apophyge

B Column variants
8 Caryatid
9 Atlanta (Telamon)
10 Fluted column
11 Spiral fluted
12 Rusticated
13 Solomonic (Salomónica) column

C Capital forms
14 Bud (Lotus)
15 Bell (Papyrus)
16 Volute
17 Palm
18 Bull
19 Foliated
20 Cushion
21 Scalloped
22 Waterleaf
23 Crocket
24 Stiff-leaf

D Column and pier forms
25 Clustered
26 Octagonal
27 Filleted
28 Compound
29 Engaged
30 Shaft ring
31 Base moulding
32 Pilaster
33 Engaged

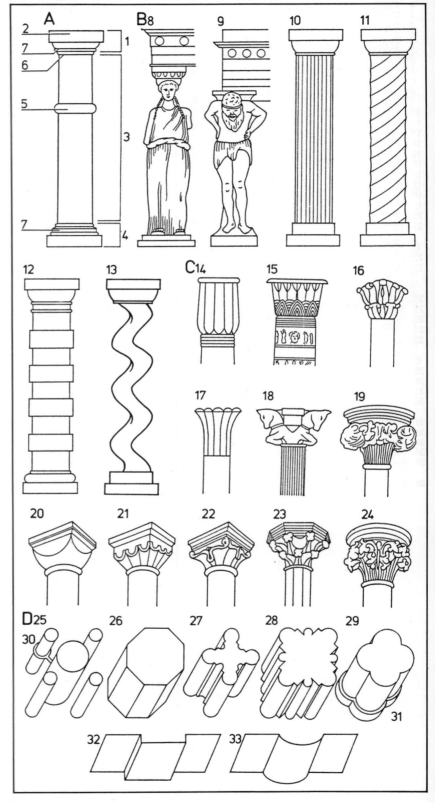

© DIAGRAM

1.07

A Castle
1 Barbican
2 Causeway
3 Palisade
4 Moat (ditch with water)
5 Watchtower
6 Drawbridge, etc
7 Postern gate (sally port)
8 Scarp
9 Outer curtain wall
   (enceinte)
10 Portcullis
11 Keep (donjon)
12 Inner bailey (ward)
13 Outer bailey (ward)
14 Gatehouse
15 Arrow slit (oeillet)
16 Angle tower
17 Flanking tower
18 Curtain wall bastion
19 Ramparts
20 Chapel
21 Garderobe

B Walls (crenellated)
22 Machicolation
23 Parapet wooden hourdes
   or brattices (overhead
   cover)
24 Embrasure (crenel)
25 Merlon
26 Rampart walk
27 Parapet
28 Corbel

C Fortress bastion features
29 Talus
30 Terreplein
31 Banquette
32 Pepperpot sentry box
   (guerite)
33 Ditch
34 Counterscarp
35 Covered way
36 Traverse
37 Ravelin (half moon/demi-
   lune)
38 Glacis

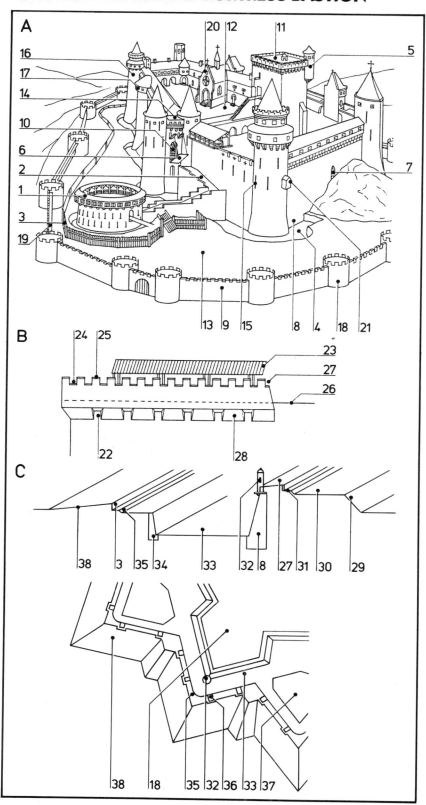

1.08

A   Roofing
1   Bell gable
2   Bartizan
3   Tower
4   Battlement
5   Pinnacles
6   Flèche
7   Spire (with tower, a steeple)
8   Broach spire
9   Needle spire
10   Weathervane
11   Octagonal spire
12   Helm
13   Campanile
14   Louvres
15   Bell cote
16   Sanctus bell
17   Crochet

B   Side features
18   Buttress
19   Flying buttress
20   Porch
21   Gargoyle
22   Spout
23   Plinth
24   Clerestory
25   Baptistery
26   Dwarf gallery

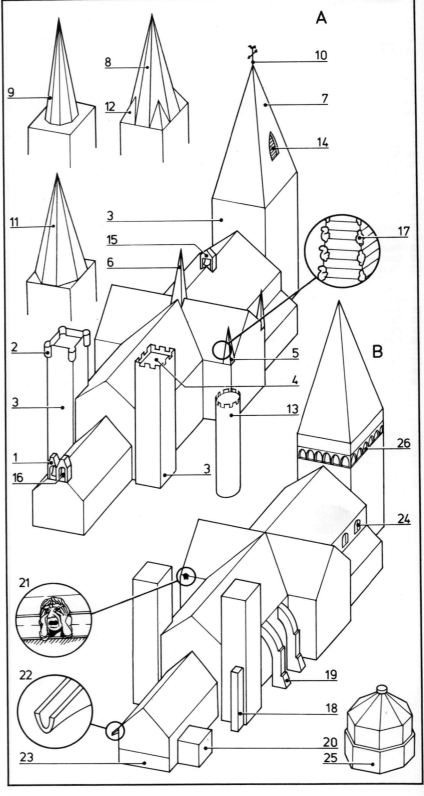

©DIAGRAM

BUILDINGS
CHURCH INTERIOR LAYOUT

A Basilican layout
1 Chapel
2 Ambulatory
3 Altar
4 Choir (chancel)
4a Crypt (below choir)
5 Crossing
6 Aisle
7 Chapel
8 Transept
8a North
8b South
9 Nave
10 Chantry chapels
11 Aisles
11a North
11b South
12 Porch
13 Lady chapel
14 Presbytery/Sanctuary
15 Sacristy/Vestry
16 Chapterhouse
17 Cloister
18 Galilee porch
19 Parclose screen
20 Chancel screen
21 Slype

B Greek cross (Byzantine) layout
22 Atrium
23 Narthex
24 Parakklesion
25 Apse
26 Bema
27 Iconostasis
28 Tribune
29 Pastrophory

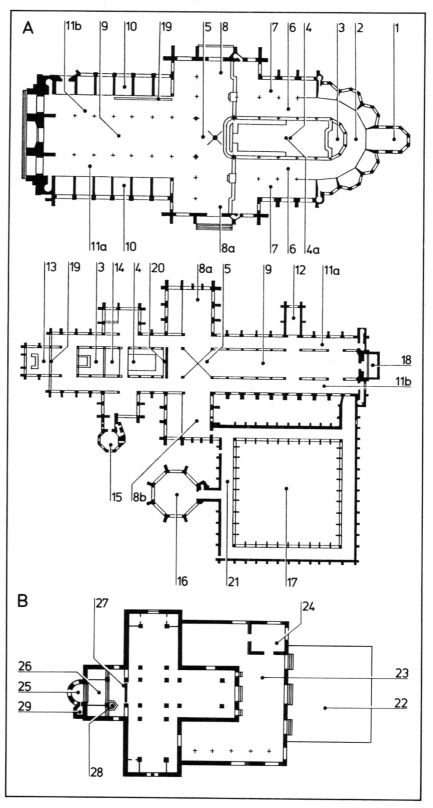

1 Altar and altar rail
2 Almonry/Aumbry
3 Brasses
4 Clerestory
5 Easter sepulchre
6 Font
7 Funeral hatchments
8 Gargoyle
9 Lectern
10 Misericord seat
11 Pew, stall
12 Piscina
13 Pulpit (Ambo)
14 Reredos
15a Rood
15b Roodscreen
16 Sanctuary knocker
17 Screens (parclose)
18 Sedilia
19 Stoup
20 Triforium
21 Squint (hagioscope)
22 Canopy
23 Choir screen
24 Credence (credenza)

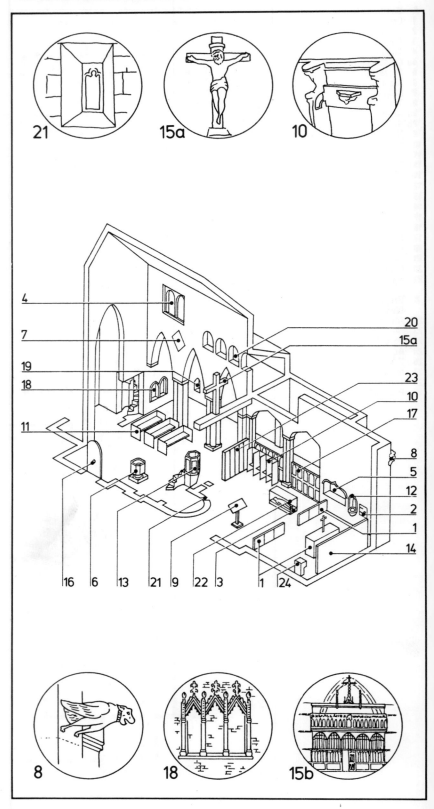

©DIAGRAM

A **Window types**
1 Light
2 Shaft
3 Mullion
4 Transom
5 Lancet
6 Tracery
7 Plate tracery
8 Foil
9 Cusp
10 Cusping
11 Dagger
12 Mouchette
13 Trefoil
14 Quatrefoil
15 Multifoil
16 Rose (Catherine wheel, compass)

B **Tracery forms**
17 Geometrical
18 Intersecting
19 Panel
20 Reticulated
21 Curvilinear (flowing)

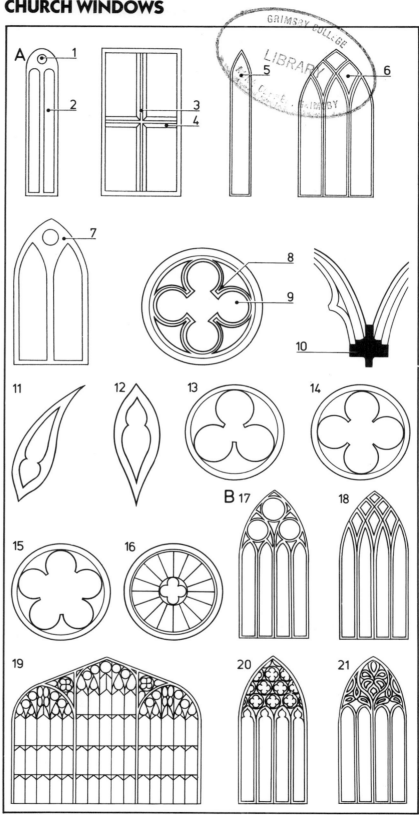

1.12

BUILDINGS
CHURCH WALL PARTS

A Wall surface
1 Kneeler
2 Band
3 Arcade
4 String course/Stringer
5 Hood mould
6 Champfer (splay)
6a Stop champfer
7 Flush work
8 'Long and short' work
9 Coping
10 Cavity
11 Cornice
12 Sill
13 Bracket
14 Footing
15 Niche
16 Laced arches
17 Spandrel

B Buttresses
18 Buttress
19 Flying buttress
20 Set off
21 Blocking
22 Diagonal

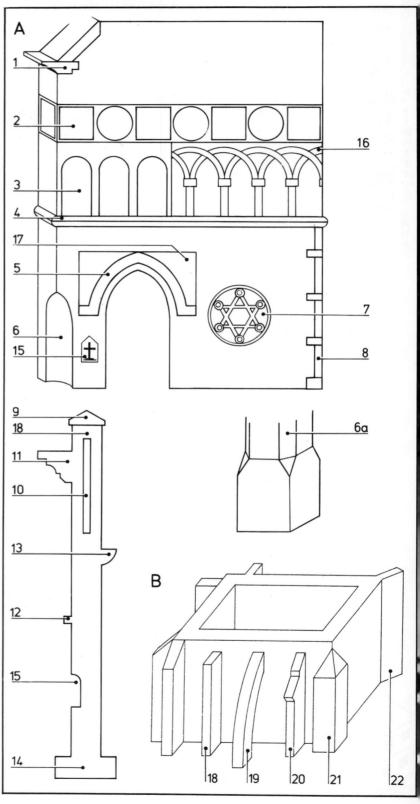

©DIAGRAM

1.13

A **Upper floor (2nd storey)**
1 Solar
2 Staircase
3 Ladder to loft dormitory
4 Loft dormitory
5 Roof
6 Chimney

B **Lower floor (1st storey)**
7 Store (cellar)
8 Hall
9 Fireplace hearth
10 Steps
11 Front door
12 Kitchen
13 Passage
14 Buttery
15 Pantry
16 Privy

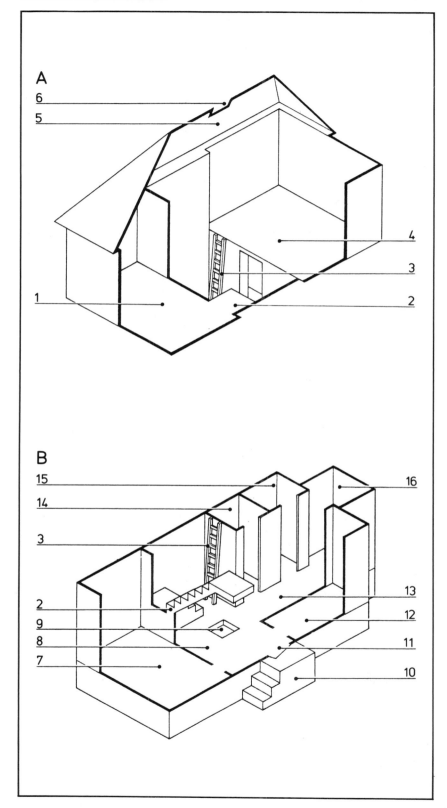

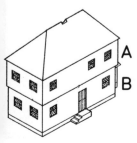

1.14

A Second floor/Attic (3rd storey)
1 Servants' quarters
2 Box room

B First floor (2nd storey)
3 Gentleman's bedroom
4 Gentleman's dressing room
5 Lady's bedroom
6 Boudoir (lady's dressing room)
7 Nursery
8 Bathroom and toilet
9 Landing
10 Guest bedroom
11 Staircase

C Ground floor (1st storey)
12 Hall
13 Parlour
14 Dining room
15 Kitchen
16 Scullery
17 Pantry
18 Breakfast room
19 Drawing room
20 Toilet
21 Library/Smoking room
22 Front porch
23 Conservatory
24 Music room

D Basement
25 Wine cellar
26 Storage room
27 Coal store
28 Basement steps

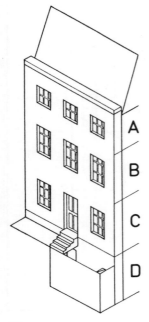

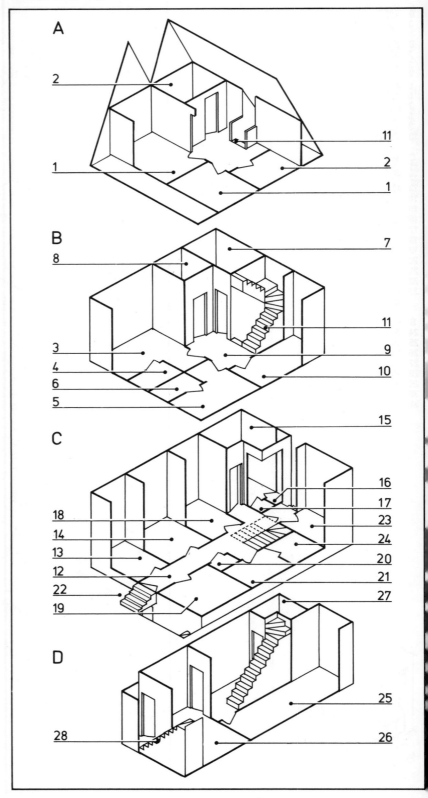

©DIAGRAM

1.15

BUILDINGS
MODERN HOUSE

A Loft/attic
1 Loft door

B First floor (2nd storey)
2 Master bedroom
3 Dummy breast
4 Ensuite bathroom
5 Bathroom and toilet
6 Nursery
7 Second bedroom
8 Guest bedroom
9 Landing
10 Stairs to ground floor

C Ground floor (1st storey)
11 Stairs to first floor
12 Front door
13 Hallway
14 Lounge/Living room
15 Fireplace
16 Dining room
17 Conservatory/Sun lounge
18 Breakfast bar
19 Kitchen
20 Back door
21 Pantry/Larder
22 Toilet
23 Door and stairs to basement

D Basement/Cellar
24 Stairs to ground floor
25 Passage
26 Laundry room
27 Garage
28 Workshop/Hobby room
29 Wine cellar
30 Storage cupboard
31 Garage door

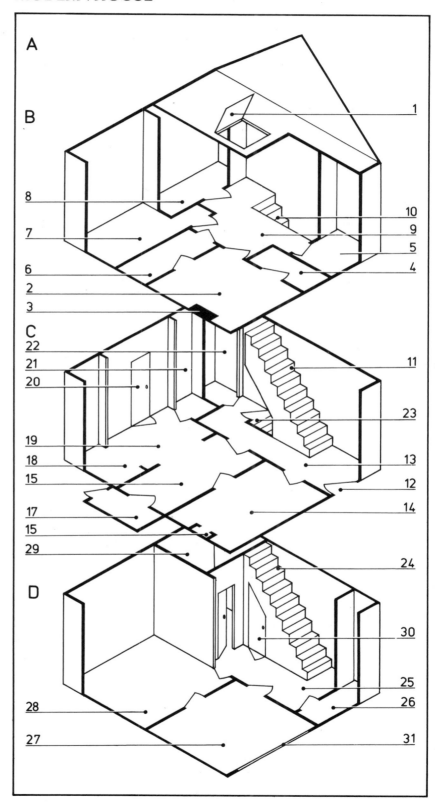

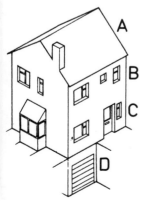

A Basic arrangements (ancient)
1 Rubblework (dry stone masonry)
2 Rag-work (ragstone)
3 Ashlar (regular)/Opus quadratum
4 Polygonal (cyclopean)

B Basic arrangements (modern)
5 Random
6 Random coursed
7 Broken coursed
8 Irregular coursed

C Roman stonework
9 Polygonal
10 Opus incertum
11 Opus reticulatum
12 Opus testaceum

D Stone dressing
13 Pointed
14 Broached
15 Rusticated
16 Vermiculated

E Stone positions
17 Natural bedded
18 Edge bedded
19 Face bedded
20 Chequer work

F Stone edgings
21 Footings
22 Quoin (coign)
23 Coping

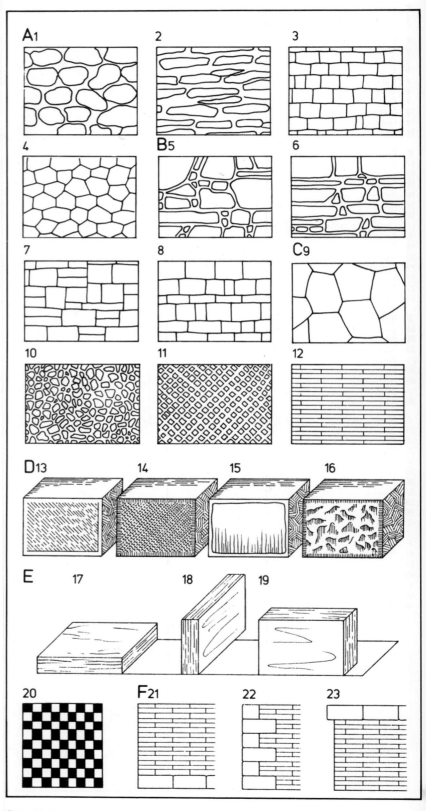

©DIAGRAM

2.02

A Parts of a brick
1 Bed
2 Frog
3 Side
4 Face
5 Cull
6 End
7 Bat (half)
8 Three quarters
9 Closer
10 King closer
11 Queen closer
12 Split (soap)

B Positions of a brick
13 Stretcher
14 Header
15 Soldier
16 Sailor
17 Bull (rowlock) header
18 Bull stretcher

C Varieties of brick
19 Stock
20 Air
21 Brindled
22 Compass
23 Gauged (brick & brick)
24 Norman

D Wall thickness
25 3in (Bull stretcher face)
26 4in (Stretcher face)
27 13½in (Cavity wall with metal tie)
28 9in (Header face)
29 13½in (Brick-and-a-half wall)
30 9in (Rowlock back)

E Mortar joints
31 Weathered
32 Concave or rodded
33 'V' shaped
34 Extruded
35 Beaded
36 Ruler
37 Flush or plain cut
38 Flush + rodded
39 Struck
40 Raked

F Metal ties
41 Rectangular
42 'Z' shape
43 Adjustable 'Z' shape
44 Mesh
45 Corrugated
46 Butterfly

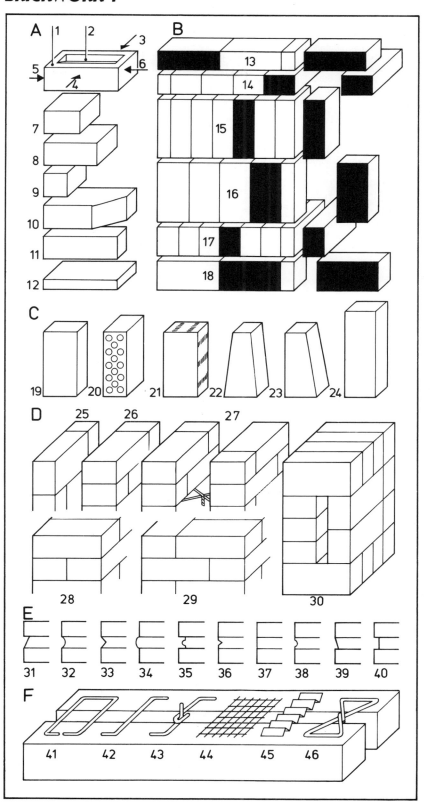

2.03

STRUCTURES
BRICKWORK 2

1 **Running bond**
2 ⅓ Running bond
3 Stack bond
4 American/Scotch/English garden wall bond
5 English bond (Dutch)
6 Flemish bond (Dutch)
7 Common (6th course headers)
8 Common (6th course Flemish headers)
9 Flemish spiral
10 Flemish cross
11 Flemish diagonal
12 Flemish double header
13 Rat-trap
14 Flemish garden wall
15 English cross or St Andrew's cross
16 Herringbone
17 Diagonal running bond
18 Basket weave or Parquet

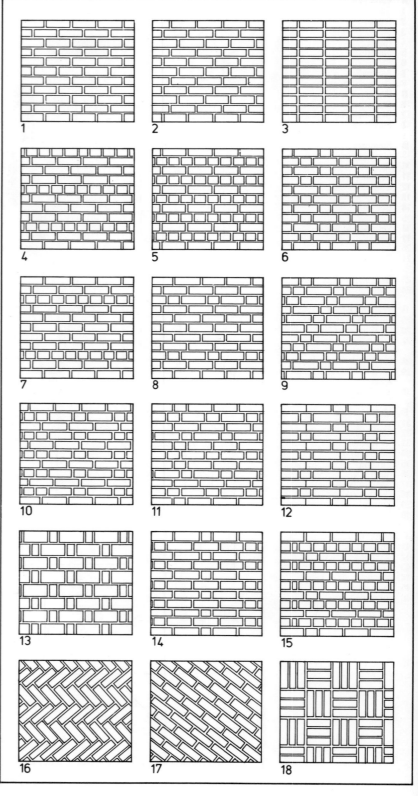

©DIAGRAM

A **Wood walls**
1 Sheathing
2 Panelling
3 Clapper board
   (clapboard,
   weatherboarding)
4 Shingle
5 Log framing

B **Wood patterns**
6 Staggered
7 Diamond
8 Fishscale
9 Chisel
10 Sawtooth

C **Wood siding**
11 Board on board
12 Board and batten
13 Tongue and groove
14 Bevelled board
15 Simple drop
16 Shiplap
17 Nogging

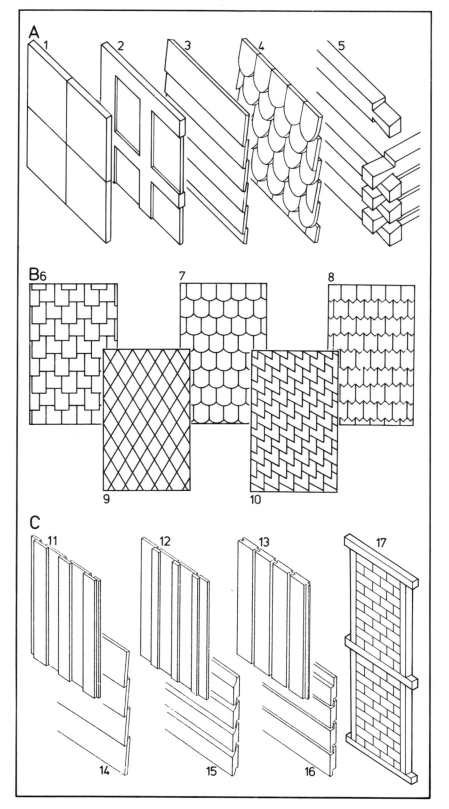

2.05

A Parts of a roof
1 Verge
2 Eave
3 Ridge
4 Gable
5 Hip
6 Valley
7 Dormer
8 Gablet
9 Skylight

B Types of roof
10 Gabled (pitched, saddleback)
11 Hipped
12 Hipped gable (jerkin head)
13 Gambrel (USA), Mansard (UK)
14 Mansard (UK and USA) (double-pitch)
15 Lean to
16 Monitor
17 Skirt
18 Saw tooth
19 Valley (m-shaped)
20 Penthouse
21 Rainbow
22 Ogee
23 Barrel
24 Flat
25 Y form
26 Hyperbolic paraboloid

C Types of turret
27 Rotunda
28 Domed
29 Imperial
30 Conical broach
31 Spired

STRUCTURES
ROOF TYPES

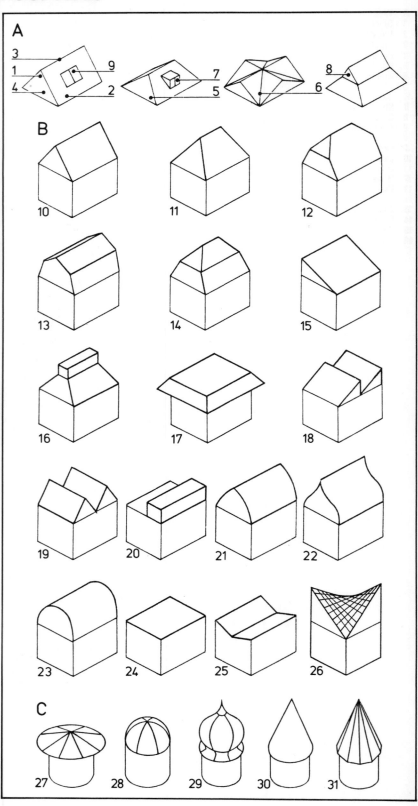

© DIAGRAM

STRUCTURES
DOMES

A Types
1 Dome (cupola)
2 Sail dome
3 Drum dome
4 Pendentive
5 Domical
6 Umbrella (parachute)

B Supports
7 Squinch arches
8 Corbelling
9 Pendentive

C Parts
10 Lantern
11 Dome (cupola)
12 Drum
13 Pendentive

D Features
14 Oculus
15 Coffer indentations
16 Attic tier/storey

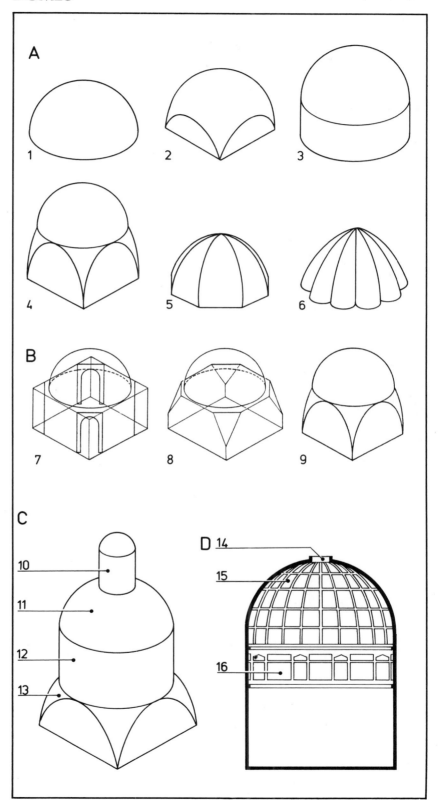

1 Barrel (wagon, tunnel)
2 Groin (cross)
3 Oblong
4 Rib
5 Transverse rib
6 Diagonal rib
7 Transverse ridge rib
8 Tiercerons
9 Squinch arch
10 Sexpartite
11 Lierne
12 Liernes
13 Fan
14 Boss
15 Pendentive

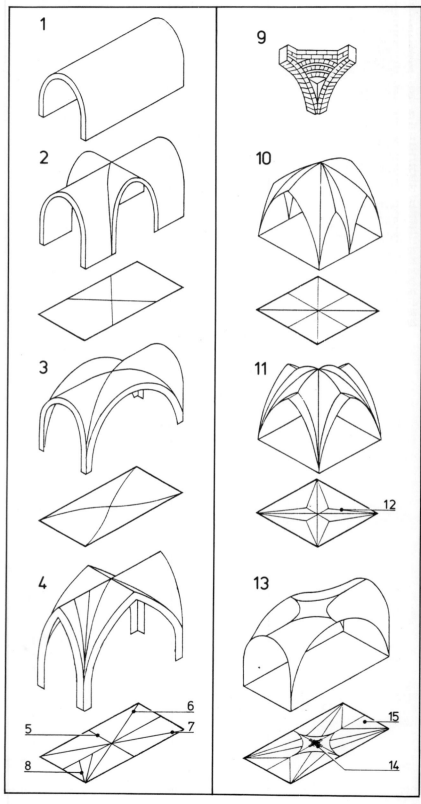

©DIAGRAM

STRUCTURES
ROOFING

A   **Types of roof surfacing**
1   Thatch
2   Plain tile
3   Pantile
4   Spanish tile
5   Slate
6   Sheeting (asphalt)
7   Corrugated
8   Interlocked
9   Bitumen felt

B   **Parts of roof**
10   Cornice
11   Barge boards
12   Cresting
13   Finial
14   Stack (chimney)
15   Pot (chimney)
16   Cowl (chimney)
17   Breast (chimney)
18   Stepped flashing
19   Ridge tiles
20   Hip flashing
21   Modillons
22   Fish scale
23   Guttering
24   Valley flashing
25   Down pipe
26   Gable
27   Shaped gable
28   Dutch gable
29   Pargetting

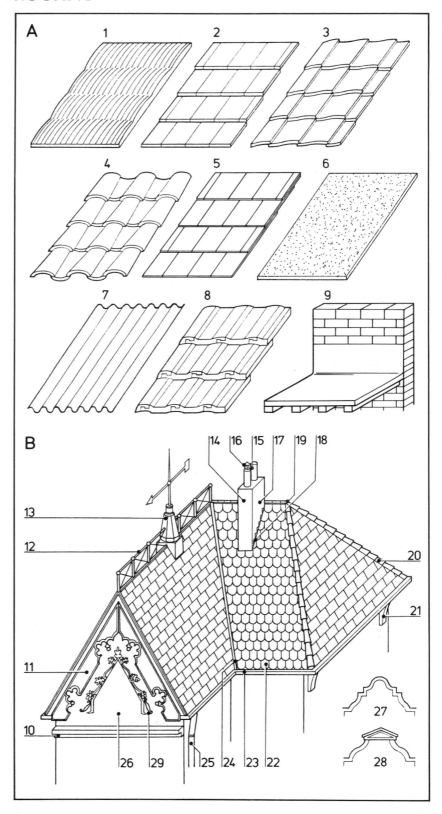

2.09

STRUCTURES
ROOF SUPPORTS

A Crucks
1 Full cruck
2 Base cruck
3 Raised cruck
4 Middle cruck
5 Upper cruck

B Trusses (traditional)
6 Tie beam
7 King post
8 Queen post
9 Crown post
10 Hammerbeam
11 Arch brace
12 Scissor brace

C Trusses (modern)
13 Flat pratt
14 Flat warren
15 Belgian (pitched)
16 Scissors
17 Clerestory

D Major roof support members
18 Ridge
19 Rafter
20 Beam
21 Purlin
22 Wall plate
23 Strut
24 Sprocket
25 Brace
26 Corbel
27 Collar
28 Dragon beam

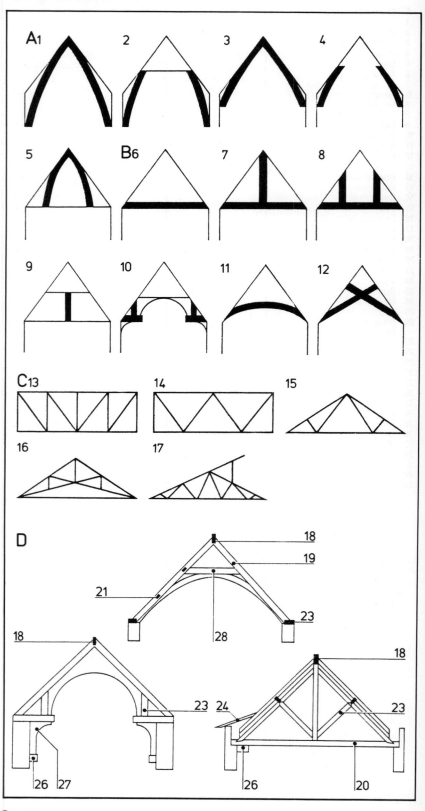

©DIAGRAM

A Wainscot
1 Cornice
2 Moulding
3 Panel
4 Dado rail
5 Dado panel
6 Skirting

B Parquet floorings
7 English
8 Dogleg
9 Hungarian
10 Brixon plank
11 Assemblage
12 Mosaic

C Parts (Balloon framing)
13 Ridge board
14 Double header
15 Double trimmer rafter
16 Common rafter
17 Collar beam gable
18 End rafter
19 Gable end stud
20 Ceiling joist
21 Plate
22 Stud
23 Cross rail (girt)
24 Floor joist
25 Cap
26 Diagonal brace (cross brace)
27 Continuous stud
28 Wood girder
29 Plinth
30 Sole plate
31 Continuous ledger
32 Wood sheathing
33 Corner post
34 Diagonal wood flooring
35 Goss bridging
36 Bottom cripple
37 Window sill
38 Ribbon
39 Firestopping
40 Top cripple
41 Window frame

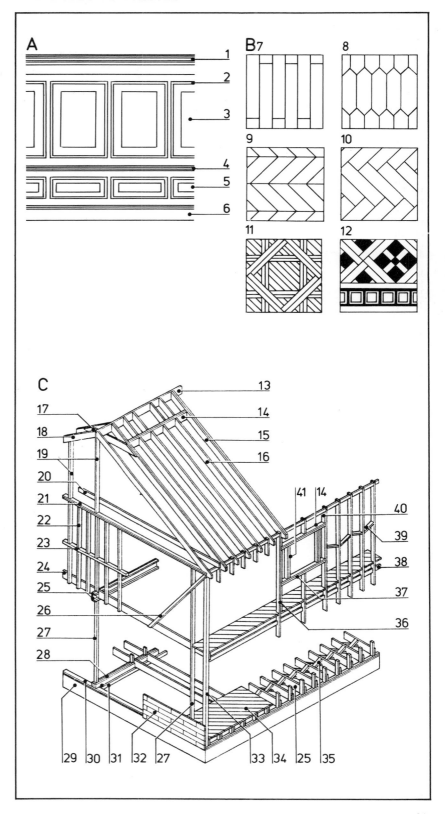

2.11

STRUCTURES
STAIRCASES

A Stair parts
1 Newel post
2 Baluster
3 Hand rail
4 Quarterpiece (landing)
5 Skirting
6 Wall stringer
7 Waist
8 Flight
9 Run (tread)
10 Riser
11 Nosing
12 Curtail step
  (bottom step)

B Types of staircase
13 Spiral (circular)
14 Quarter turn
15 Quarter winding
16 Wreath (vise)
17 Straight flight
18 Dogleg
19 Geometrical
20 Double return

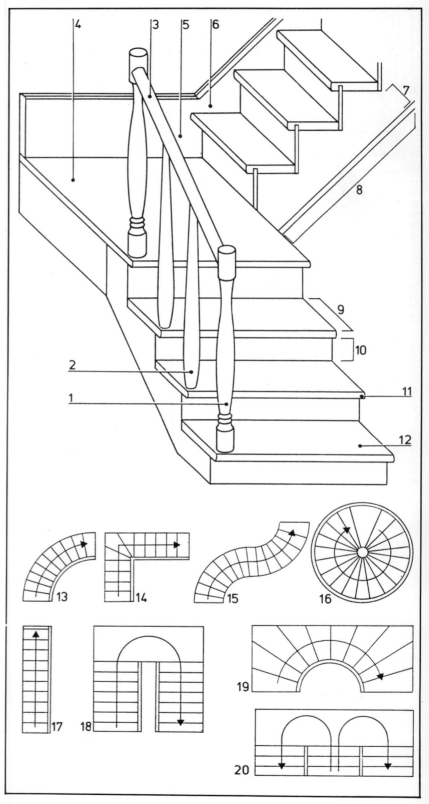

© DIAGRAM

A Geometry
1 Rise
2 Spring line
3 Span
4 Centre
5 Axis
6 Crown
7 Haunch
8 Terminal

B Elements
9 Keystone
10 Voussoir
11 Impost
12 Abutment
13 Extrados
14 Intrados (soffit)
15 Depth

C Segmental arches
16 Shoulder
17 Screwback
18 Camber

D Vaulted
19 Capstone
20 Vaultstone
21 Pendant
22 Tympanum

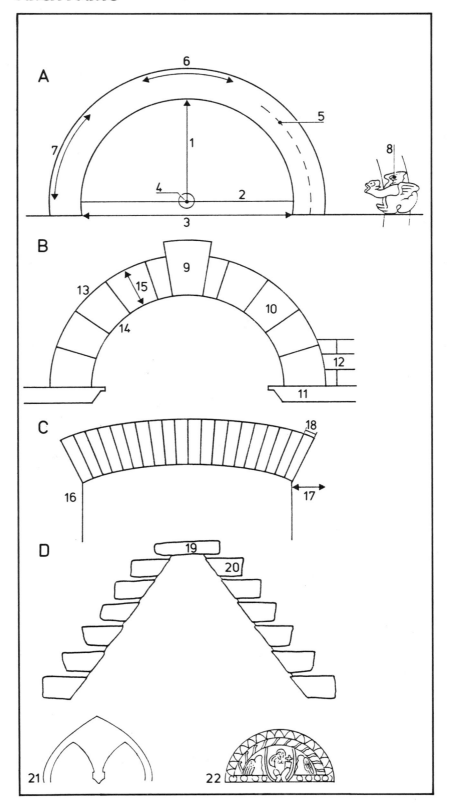

2.13

STRUCTURES
ARCH TYPES

A Circular types
1 Semi circular
2 Semi circular stilted
3 Segmental
4 Round horseshoe
5 Horseshoe
6 Three centred
7 Depressed three centred
8 Elliptical
9 Parabolic
10 Round trefoil
11 Round trifoliated
12 Pseudo three centred
13 Shouldered
14 Venetian
15 Florentine
16 Stilted

B Pointed types
17 Triangular
18 Corbelled
19 Pointed horseshoe
20 Pointed Saracenic
21 Lancet
22 Equilateral
23 Drop
24 Pointed segmental
25 Four-centred (Tudor)
26 Rampant
27 Pseudo four-centred
28 Pointed trefoil
29 Pointed trifoliated
30 Cinquefoil
31 Ogee

C Flat arch (Dutch, French, Welsh, Jack, USA)

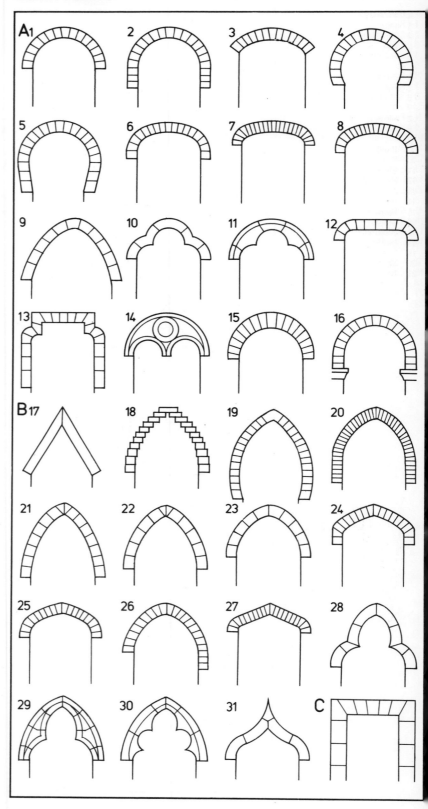

©DIAGRAM

2.14

STRUCTURES
WINDOW PARTS

A Protruding windows
1 Box
2 Bay/Bow
3 Bay curved
4 Barrel

B Roof windows
5 Rooflight
6 Eyebrow
7 Gabled dormer
8 Hipped dormer
9 Oriel

C Parts
10 Hood
11 Sill (apron)
12 Header (head frame)
13 Jamb
14 Hanging stile
15 Pane
16 Glazing bar
17 Weatherboard
18 Mullion (muntin)
19 Sash frame
20 Shutters Jalousie
21 Transom

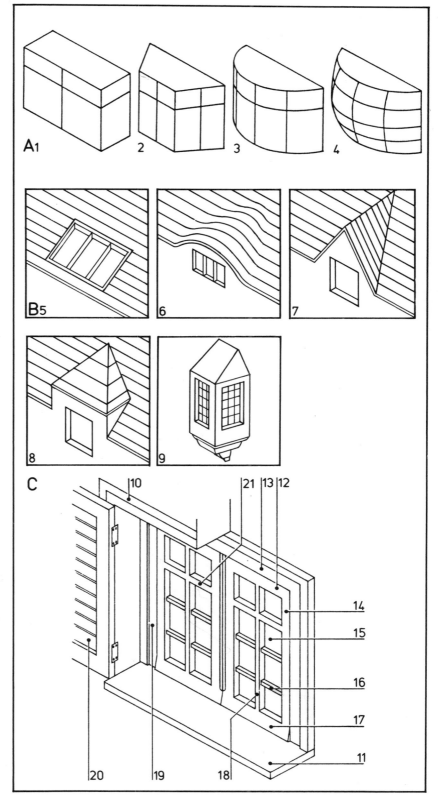

© DIAGRAM

35

2.15

STRUCTURES
WINDOW TYPES

© DIAGRAM

2.16

STRUCTURES
DOOR PARTS

A Door fixtures
1 Bolt lock
2 Chain lock
3 Key hole
4 Latch
5 Box handle
6 Door knob
7 Hinge
8 Eye (spy hole)
9 Push plate

B Door parts
10 Architrave
11 Top rail
12 Shutting stile
13 Hanging stile
14 Top panel
15 Muntin
16 Lock rail
17 Middle panel
18 Bottom panel
19 Bottom rail (plinth block)

C Door parts
20 Cornice
20a Lintel
21 Header
22 Jamb
23 Hinge
24 Weatherboard
25 Threshold

D Porch and entry
26 Curved brackets
27 Porch posts
28 Front steps
29 Wooden balustrade
30 Masonry stoop
31 Fan light
32 Canopy

E Hands of doors
33 Left hand reverse
34 Left hand
35 Right hand
36 Right hand reverse

F Meeting profiles
37 Rabbeted
38 Bullnose
39 Parallel bevel

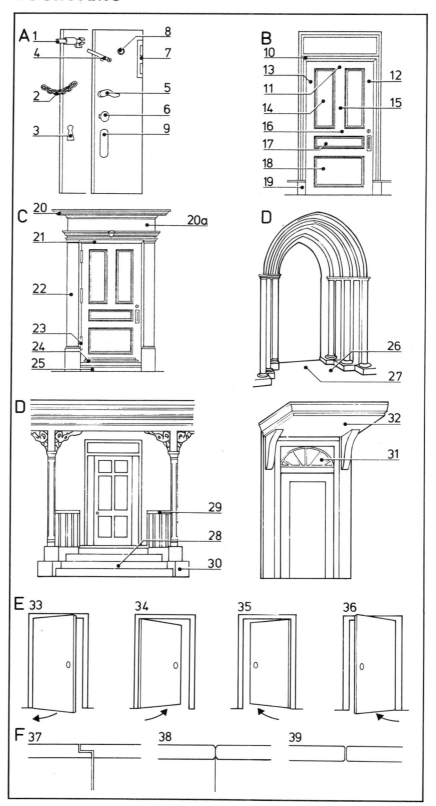

2.17

1 Flush
2 Panel
3 Glass
4 Ledge and brace
5 Dutch (stable)
6 Screen
7 Louvred
8 French
9 Hanging
10 Revolving
11 Swing
12 Double swing
13 Sliding
14 Double slide
15 Accordion
16 Folding
17 Roll
18 Turnstile

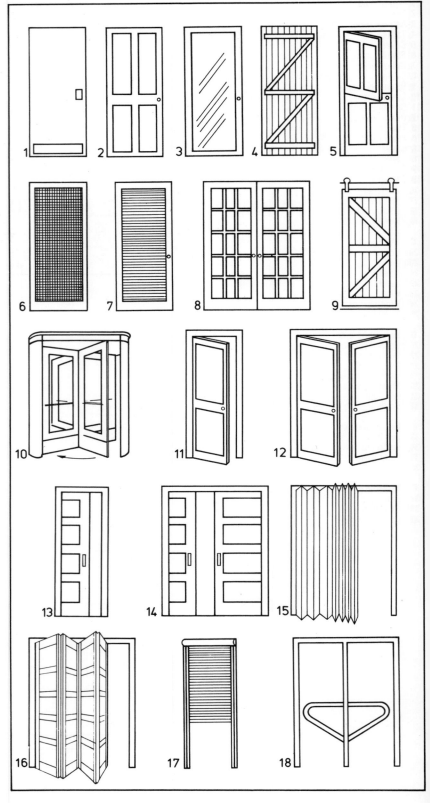

©DIAGRAM

3.01

1 Fillet raised
2 Fillet sunk
3 Astragel (baguette)
4 Torus
5 Cavetto (cone)
6 Scotia
7 Hollow
8 Ovolo
9 Round (bowtell)
10 Cyma recta
11 Cyma reversa
12 Beak
13 Thumb
14 Fascia
15 Bevel
16 Quirk
17 Chamfered
18 Thumbnail bead

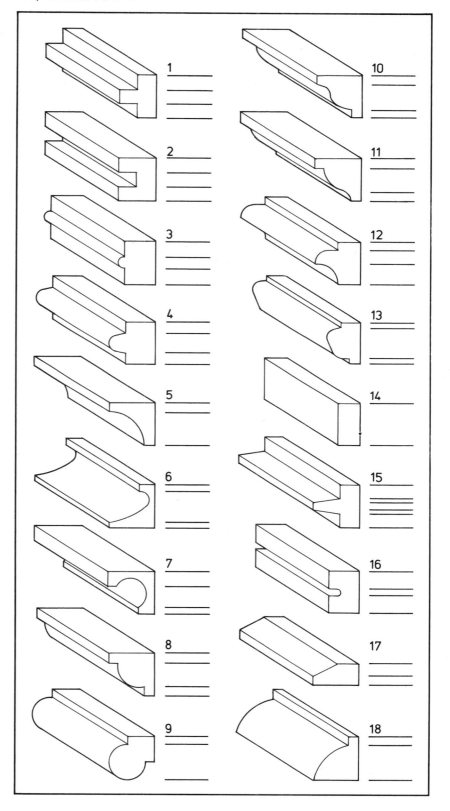

3.02

ORNAMENT
MOULDINGS 2

1 Cock bead
2 Rope torus/Twisted cord (cable)
3 Fluted torus
4 Reeded torus
5 Reed and tie
6 Quirk bead
7 Dentil
8 Flush bead
9 Scroll
10 Keel
11 Nailhead
12 Ogee
13 Reverse ogee
14 Corona
15 Billet
16 Bead and reel
17 Beaded
18 Nebuly/Nebulé

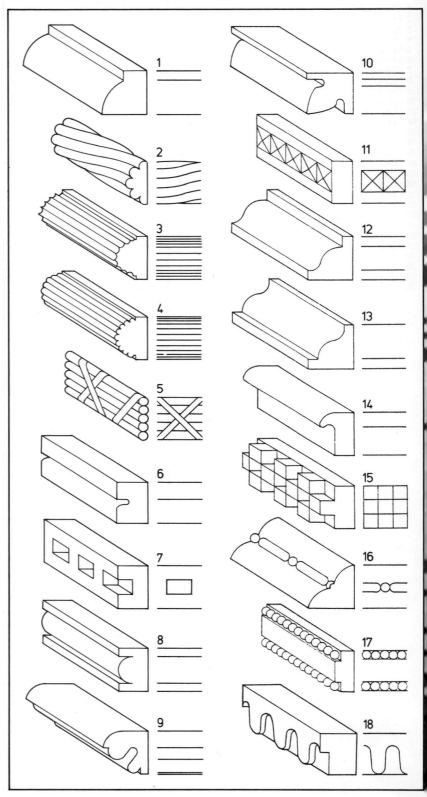

© DIAGRAM

ORNAMENT
MOTIFS 1

1 Reeding
2 Fluting
3 Linenfold
4 Key
5 Fret
6 Fret
7 Continuous coil spiral
8 Dentil
9 Square billet
10 Round billet
11 Chevron
12 Chevron
13 Zig zag
14 Peardrop
15 Wave
16 Wave
17 Double cone
18 Bead
19 Reel
20 Beed and reel
21 Gadroon
22 Grape
23 Guttae
24 Egg and dart
25 Egg and tongue
26 Nailhead
27 Dog tooth
28 Tablet flower

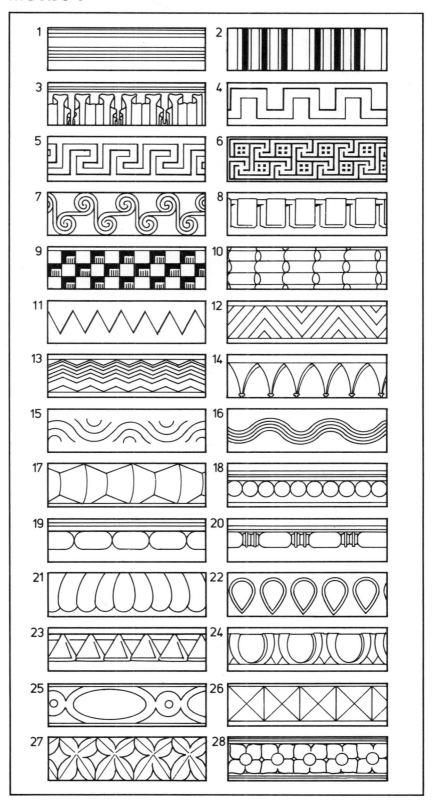

3.04

1 Herringbone
2 Lozenge
3 Chain
4 Ball flower
5 Rose
6 Beakhead
7 Rope (cable)
8 Bay leaf garland
9 Rope and feather
10 Vitruvian scroll (running dog)
11 Guilloche
12 Guilloche
13 Guilloche
14 Scroll (leaf)
15 Scroll (leaf and rose)
16 Vignette
17 Papyrus
18 Festoon
19 Water leaf and tongue
20 Water leaf and dart
21 Lunette
22 Lotus
23 Lotus and papyrus
24 Anthemion
25 Acanthus
26 Anthemion and palmette
27 Anthemion and palmette
28 End scroll (volute)

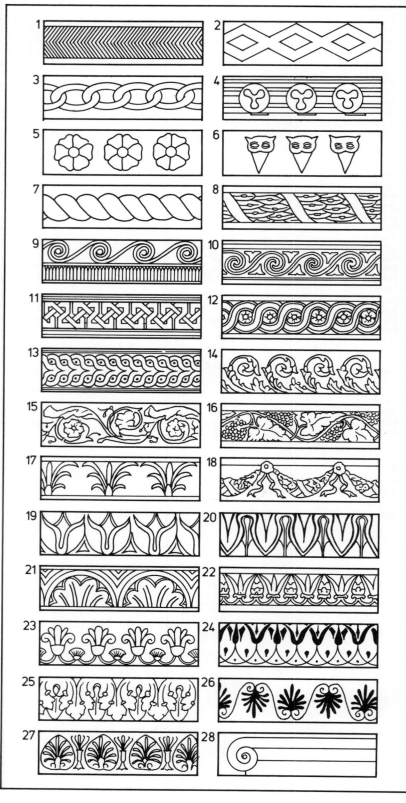

©DIAGRAM

3.05

ORNAMENT
DEVICES 1

1 Lion rampant
2 Lion statant
3 Lion rampant guardant
4 Lion passant
5 Lion statant
6 Lion passant guardant
7 Lion sejant
8 Lion sejant rampant
9 Lion couchant
10 Lion salient
11 Lion coward
12 Lion queue fourchée
13 Demi-lion
14 Lion's head
15 Lion's face
16 Lion's paw couped
17 Stag at gaze
18 Stag trippant
19 Stag at speed
20 Stag's head cabossed
21 Leopard's face
22 Boar rampant
23 Boar's head couped
24 Horse rampant
25 Bear's head couped
26 Dog rampant
27 Martlet
28 Pelican
29 Eagle displayed
30 Two headed eagle
31 Vol
32 Griffin
33 Wyvern
34 Dragon
35 Serpent nowed
36 Serpent vorant
37 Cockatrice
38 Fish hauriant
39 Dolphin
40 Two dolphins
41 Escallop
42 Garb
43 Fir trees eradicated
44 Oak tree on mount
45 Seiren
46 Mermaid
47 Triquetra
48 Appaumée
49 Patera
50 Bucranium

©DIAGRAM

43

1 Greek cross
2 Latin cross
3 Tau cross
4 Quadrate cross
5 Patriarchal cross/
   Cross of Lorraine
6 Pointed cross
7 Fourchée cross
8 St Andrew's cross
9 Double Cross
10 Forked cross
11 Papal cross
12 Cross crosslet
13 Cross moline
14 Cross recercellée
15 Cross fleurettée
16 Cross pommée
17 Cross patée
18 Maltese cross
19 Cross cramponée
20 Cross botonée
21 Fylfot
22 Cross avellane
23 Cross potent
24 Cross fimbriated
25 Fivefold cross
26 Crescent
27 Increscent
28 Decrescent
29 Mullet
30 Star
31 Mullet pierced
32 Estoile
33 Trefoil slipped
34 Quatrefoil
35 Cinquefoil
36 Rose-en-soleil
37 Fleurs-de-lis
38 Catherine wheel
39 Caltrap
40 Bowen knot
41 Bourchier knot
42 Stafford knot
43 Heneage knot
44 Wake knot
45 Acanthus

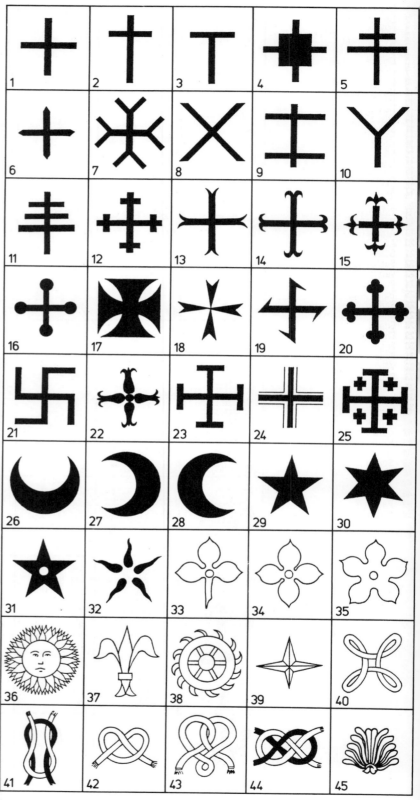

©DIAGRAM

A **Parts of a shield**
1 The field
2 Chief
3 Dexter
4 Sinister
5 Base
6 Dexter chief
7 Middle chief
8 Sinister chief
9 Dexter base
10 Fess point
11 Sinister fess
12 Dexter base
13 Sinister base
14 Middle base
15 Honour
16 Fess
17 Nombril

B **Tinctures**
18 Or (gold)
19 Argent (silver)
20 Azure (blue)
21 Gules (red)
22 Sable (black)
23 Vert (green)
24 Purpure (purple)
25 Tenné (orange-tawny)
26 Sanguine (blood red)
27 Murrey (mulberry red)
28 Ermine
29 Erminois
30 Ermines
31 Pean
32 Vair
33 Counter vair
34 Vair en point
35 Potent
36 Counter potent

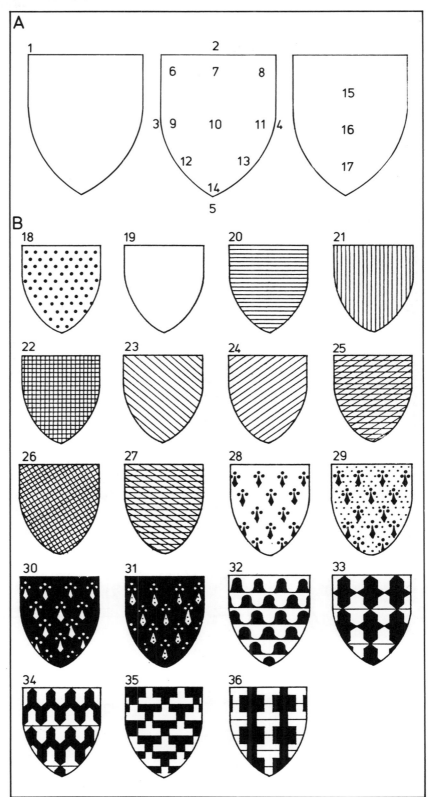

A Divisions of field
1 Per pale
2 Per fess
3 Per bend
4 Per bend sinister
5 Per saltire
6 Per pall
7 Per chevron
8 Per cross
9 Gyronny (8 piece)
10 Gyronny (6 piece)
11 Per pale sinister half per fess
12 Per fess per pale
13 Bar in fess
14 Bar in pale
15 Bar in bend
16 Barry
17 Bendy
18 Bendy sinister
19 Paly
20 Chevronny
21 Checky
22 Lozengy
23 Fusily
24 Barry bendy
25 Paly bendy
26 Company
27 Per pale and barry
28 Bezanty
29 Goutty
30 Semy de lys

B Division-line types
31 Engrailed
32 Invected
33 Wavy or undy
34 Wavy or undy
35 Nebuly
36 Nebuly
37 Indented
38 Dancetty
39 Embattled
40 Raguly
41 Dovetailed
42 Potenty
43 Angled
44 Bevelled
45 Escartelly
46 Nowy
47 Embattled grady
48 Arched
49 Double arched
50 Urdy
51 Floretty
52 Dancetty floretty
53 Crested
54 Rayonny

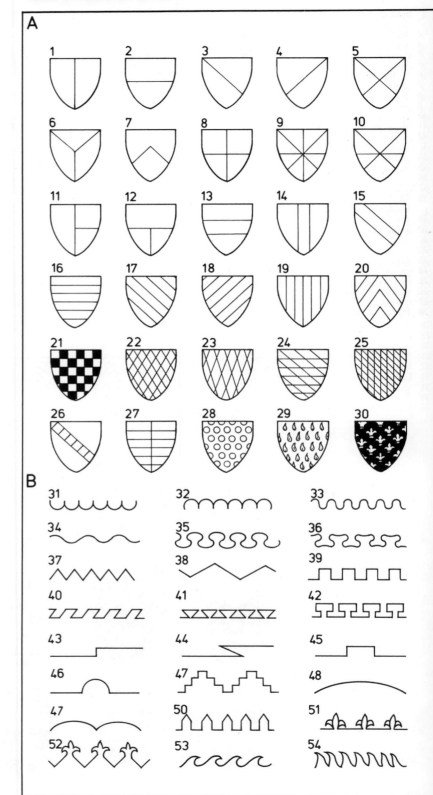

3.09

DECORATIONS
HERALDIC DEVICES 3

Charges
1 Canton
2 Gyron
3 Lozenge
4 Mascle
5 Fusil
6 Rustre
7 Billet
8 Roundel barry wavy
9 Label
10 Inescutcheon
11 Roundel
12 Annulet
13 Orle
14 Escutcheon
15 Bordure
16 Bordure embattled
17 Double tressure
18 Double tressure flory and counter flory
19 Flaunches
20 Flasques
21 Fret
22 Fretty
23 Calvary cross
24 Formy fitchy cross
25 Tau or St Anthony cross
26 Quarter pierced cross
27 Voided cross
28 Parted or Fretty cross

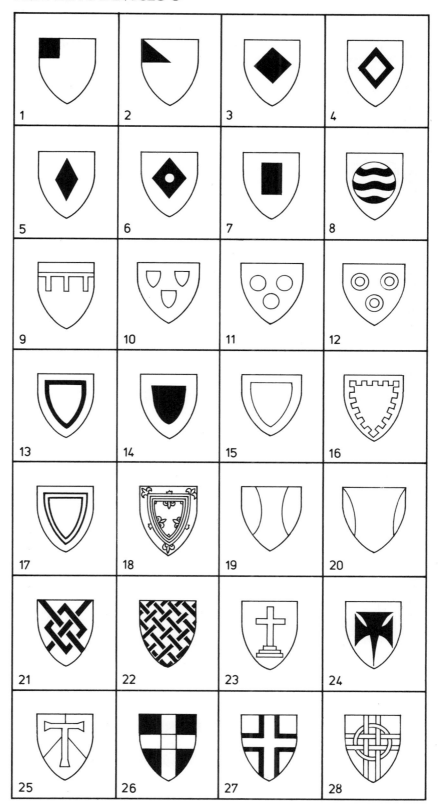

© DIAGRAM

47

3.10

A Axonometric (single view)
1 Isometric
2 Dimetric
3 Trimetric

B Plan and elevation (multi-view)

C Oblique

D Perspective (scenographic)
4 Parallel (1-point)
5 Angular (2-point)
6 Oblique (3-point)

DRAWING PROJECTIONS

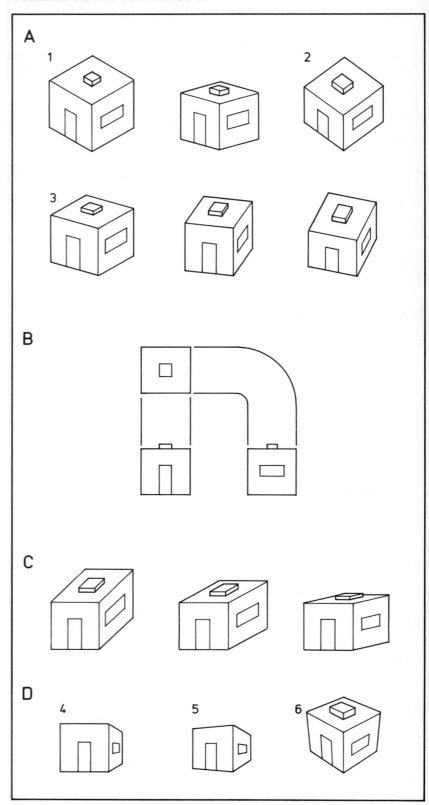

©DIAGRAM

Aalto, Hugo Alvar Henrik [1898-1976]: Finnish architect, worked in the International Modern style, with a real feeling for raw materials, especially wood and brick. Also invented bent plywood furniture.

Abacus (1.03, 1.06): a flat area at the top of a capital, dividing a column from its entablature.

Abutment (2.11): masonry surrounding and supporting the springing of an arch.

Acanthus (1.05, 3.04): a prickly leaved plant common in Greece, represented in stylized form on Corinthian capitals and throughout medieval carving.

Accordion door (2.16): a folding door.

Accordion window (2.14): a folding window.

Achievement of Arms: a display 'on a shield' of all an armigerous person's armorial bearings.

Acropolis: a hilltop citadel, especially in ancient Greece, and most notably in Athens, containing the most splendid temples and treasuries.

Acroterion (1.03): a pedestal on the apex or sides of a pediment supporting a statue or ornamental figure.

Adam, Robert [1728-92]: Scottish neoclassical architect and furniture designer. With his brother James, created the Adam style, a specifically British Georgian re-interpretation of classical architecture and interior design.

Adobe: Spanish word for a sun-dried brick common in ancient cultures and especially in arid lands. Particularly associated with the house building of the Pueblo Indians in the South West USA and Mexico.

Adyton/Adytum (1.01): the innermost and holiest room of a Greek temple.

Aedicule: small shrine or tabernacle of wood or stone, framed by columns and surmounted by an entablature and pediment.

Aerated concrete/Cellular concrete: cement-based insulating material commonly used in modern construction.

African mahogany: American hardwood.

Aggregate: a mixture of inert materials such as gravel and sand used in the make-up of plaster and concrete.

Agora: an ancient Greek market or open air assembly place.

Air brick (2.02): perforated brick used for ventilation purposes.

Air conditioning: in modern construction, the creation of an artificially controlled atmosphere within a building in isolation from external weather conditions. Particularly prevalent in very hot or cold countries.

Air shaft/Light well: an open roofless area inside a large building to provide lighting and ventilation.

Aisle (1.09): the side division of the nave of a church or basilica.

Alae (1.01): small alcoves around the sides of the atrium of a Roman house.

Alberti, Leon Battista [1404-72]: Florentine poet, scholar, architect, mathematician and compiler of treatises on the arts. Leading Italian Renaissance architect and theorist.

Alder: birch wood.

Almery: a church cupboard used either for the storage of alms or for the Sacrament.

Almonry/Aumbry (1.10): a room used especially for the distribution of alms.

Almshouse: charitable housing.

Altar (1.09, 1.10): table or slab used for the central act of sacrifice in a temple or church.

Altar rail (1.10): low, often decorated railing separating the chancel from

Acropolis: Athens after 27BC

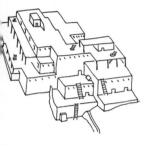
Adobe village: North Pueblo Pecos, New Mexico c1300–1700

Aedicule: Pompeii before AD79

Agora: Athens AD150

the rest of the church.

Altar-tomb: flat topped tomb in the shape of an altar.

Alure: a passageway or gallery behind a parapet.

Ambo (1.09): a type of pulpit common in Early Christian and Byzantine church architecture.

Ambulatory (1.09): the continuation of the aisle of a church surrounding the apse.

American/Common bond (2.03): a type of brick walling.

Amorino: in classical decoration a cherub or angel.

Amphiprostyle (1.03): a temple with columns and a portico at each end.

Amphitheatre: an open-air, round or oval theatre with rising rows of seating.

Altar-tomb: Porlock, England
c1500

Ancones: (a) consoles supporting a cornice over a door. (b) projections on pieces of masonry used for moving the stone and left after completion of the building.

Androne: (a) passage/corridor (1.01). (b) ancient Greek male rooms.

Angel beam: a hammerbeam (2.08) decorated with a carved angel.

Angle bonds: bonding with brickwork or metal ties at foundation level.

Angle joint: corner joint between two pieces of timber.

Angle rafter: rafter defining angle of a hip roof.

Angle tie: horizontal piece of timber which ties the wall plates at the corner of a building.

Angle tower (1.07): tower at the conjunction of fortified walls.

Angled (3.08): a division line in heraldry.

Anglo-Saxon (see style timechart): architectural style in Britain from c650 to 11th century. Most early buildings were of wood and have disappeared. More developed church architecture with towers decorated with pilaster stripes still being produced after the Norman Conquest.

Amphitheatre: Colosseum,
Rome AD82

Angular projection (3.10): a type of perspective drawing.

Annulet (1.03, 1.05, 3.09): a decorative moulded ring or band used in Greek, Romanesque and Gothic architecture.

Anta: a corner pilaster with a base and capital different from the classical order used in the rest of the building.

Antefixa: decorative marble or terra-cotta blocks used to hide the ends of the tiles on the lower edge of classical buildings.

Anthemion: honeysuckle or palmette ornament used in classical architecture and decoration.

Anthemion and palmette (3.04): see Anthemion.

Anthemius of Tralles: 6th century Byzantine architect and geometrician who, with Isidore of Miletus, designed and built one of the greatest centrally planned churches of Christendom – Hagia Sophia (532–7) at Constantinople.

Apartment house: American term for a block of flats, or building containing multiple dwelling units with a common entrance and services.

Apex stone: stone crowning the top of a gable, dome or vault.

Apodyterium (1.02): undressing room in Roman baths.

Apollodorus of Damascus [active c98–c130]: Syrian-born Roman engineer and architect who was official architect to the Emperor Trajan. Worked throughout the Empire, most notably in Rome with the Baths of Trajan and Trajan's Forum.

Apophyge (1.06): a slight expansion at the top and bottom of classical columns joining the shaft with the capital and the fillet.

Apotheca (1.01): store room in a Roman house, often on an upper floor.

Anglo-Saxon Church tower:
Earls Barton, England c1000

©DIAGRAM

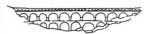

Aqueduct: Pont du Gard, Nîmes, France c19BC by Agrippa

Arabesque: by Jean Gourmont d1551

Art Deco: Chrysler Building, New York 1930 by Van Alen

Art Nouveau: Casa Milá apartment block, Barcelona, Spain 1910 by Gaudi

Applied column: see Engaged column.

Apron: (a) a projecting board inside a room below a window (2.14). (b) the overhang on a roof.

Apse (1.09): the semi-circular end of a classical building or Christian church.

Aqueduct: an elevated masonry or brick artificial channel for carrying water, widely used by the Romans.

Arabesque (3.03): generic term for intricate and subtle surface decoration based on a mixture of geometrical patterns, elaborate botanical forms and classical objects.

Araeostyle (1.05): a system of columniation in which the intervals between columns are 3½ times the column's diameter.

Arcade (1.12): a line of arches supported by pillars or columns, which can either be freestanding or attached to a building (blind arcading).

Arch (2.12, 2.13): basic architectural structure made up of wedge-shaped blocks, framing an opening, and supported from the sides only.

Arch brace (2.09): a timber truss.

Arch-brick (2.12): see Voussoir.

Archer, Thomas [1678–1743]: the only English Baroque architect to study this style in France and Italy; only practised 1703–15.

Architrave (1.03): in classical architecture the lowest of the three divisions of a beam, or entablature.

Archivolt: a moulded architrave following the contour of an arch.

Arena: originally the central area of a Roman amphitheatre used for gladiatorial combat, hence any open-air building for public display.

Argent (3.07): heraldic term for the colour silver.

Armoured cable: electrical cable used in architecture (BX cable in USA).

Arnolfo di Cambio [c1245–1302]: Florentine sculptor and master mason involved at the start of rebuilding the Duomo in Florence from 1296.

Arrow slit/Oeillet (1.07): thin opening in fortified wall to allow defenders to shoot arrows.

Arsenal: building for manufacturing and storing armaments. Two historic examples are in Venice and the Piraeus.

Art Deco: style in the decorative arts and architecture emanating from Paris in 1925 and common in both Europe and America between the world wars. Stylised and modernist, it reconciled methods of mass production and man-made materials (such as Bakelite) with sophisticated design.

Art Nouveau: the dominant style of decoration and of avant-garde building in Europe from the 1880s to the Great War. Called *Jugendstil* in Germany and *Stile Liberty* in Italy, Art Nouveau creatively adapted sinuous natural forms in an attempt to avoid architectural and design styles based on the archaeological re-creation of the past.

Arup, Ove [1895–1988]: Danish engineer and architect who pioneered methods of concrete construction in London during the 1930s. His own growing postwar output has achieved a harmonic and creative working relationship between engineering and architectural design, as at the Mining and Metallurgy Department, Birmingham University.

Asam, Cosmas Damian [1686–1739] and **Egid, Quirin** [1692–1750]: brothers who were the leading late Baroque architects and decorators in Bavaria.

Asbestos: insulating incombustible material made of mineral crystals. Now recognised as dangerously poisonous.

Ash: a pale hardwood used for veneers but not for building work.

Ashbee, Charles Robert [1863–1942]: English architect, designer and writer, associated with the Arts and Crafts Movement, and dominant member of the Art Worker's Guild.

Ashlar (2.01): smooth faced masonry.

Asphalt roofing: roofing cover made of bitumen felt or mastic asphalt.

Assemblage (2.09): flooring pattern.

Astragal (1.05, 3.01): classical moulded band atop a column shaft.

Atlanta (1.06): Greek name for carved male figure (Latin: Telamon) used as decorative support in classical and Baroque architecture.

Atrium: (a) the central courtyard and centre of life in a Roman house (1.01). (b) a courtyard in front of an Early Christian or medieval church (1.09). (c) a daylit common space in an office development.

Attic: (a) the upper storey of a classical building. (b) a garret or small room in the roof of a house (1.14).

Attic base (1.05): the standard Vitruvian base to a classical column.

Attic tier (2.06): part of the top of a dome.

Auditorium (1.02): in a classical or modern theatre, the area designed to accommodate the audience.

Awning window (2.15): a type of window.

Axis (2.12): the straight line determining the curve and springing of an arch.

Axonometric projection (3.10): method of demonstrating the construction of a building with measured geometrical drawings in three dimensions.

Azulejos: pottery tiles glazed in brilliant colours used throughout Iberia and Latin America.

Azure: heraldic term for the colour blue.

Back door (1.15): a type of door.

Backing: in masonry and brickwork, the bricks or rubble behind the facing.

Baguette (3.01): see Astragal

Bailey (1.07): the courtyard of a castle, eg between the keep and the outer wall.

Balcony: a projecting platform on the outside of a building, or the inside of a hall, protected by a railing or baluster.

Baldacchino (1.10): a canopy over an altar, either of fabric and portable, or fixed and supported on columns.

Ball-flower (3.04): an ornamental motif.

Ballast: crude mixture of sand, grit and stones.

Balloon framing (2.10): type of timber frame house construction used in Scandinavia and the USA.

Baluster/Banister (2.11): the post or pillar supporting a handrail on a staircase, or a coping.

Balustrade: a series of balusters.

Banding (1.06): horizontal subdivision of a column or wall using profile or material change.

Banister: see Baluster.

Banquette (1.07): in military architecture, a step for infantry to stand on when firing from a covered way, trench or from behind a parapet.

Baptistery (1.08): either a separate building or the part of a church reserved for the performance of the rite of baptism.

Barbican (1.07): fortifications protecting a draw-bridge, castle entrance or fortified town gate.

Barge board/Verge board/Gable board (2.08): a sloping board, frequently decorated covering the ends of roof timbers.

Barge course/Verge course: overhanging brick coping on a gable wall.

Bar in bend (3.08): a division of a heraldic field.

Balcony: Peter the Great's Mon Plaisir cottage, Peterhof, (nr Leningrad) 1712

Baldacchino: St Peter's, Rome 1633 by Bernini

© DIAGRAM

Baroque: S. Carlo alle Quattro
Fontane, Rome, facade 1667
by Borromini

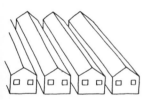

Barracks: Roman legionary
fortress after c12BC

Basilica of Maxentius
(Constantine): Rome AD313

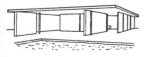

Bauhaus: German exhibition
pavilion, Barcelona 1929 by
Mies van der Rohe

Bar in fess (3.08): a division of a heraldic field.

Bar in pale (3.08): a division of a heraldic field.

Barn-door hanger: in America a garage or barn-door operated by weight carrying pulleys.

Baroque: the dominant European style of architecture and decoration to emerge from the late Renaissance at the end of the 16th century. Its component parts comprised classical forms and motifs transformed by an exuberance and richness of decoration, spatial complexity, weight and complex use of existing space and vista. Still prevalent in parts of Europe well into the 18th century.

Barracks: block accommodation for the military since Roman times.

Barrel roof (2.07): simple tunnelled roof structure.

Barrel vault (2.07): the vault inside a Barrel roof.

Barrel window (2.14): a barrel-shaped type of window.

Barry bendy (3.08): a division of a heraldic field.

Bar-tracery: see Tracery.

Bartizan (1.08): a small turret in a fortification.

Base: (a) in heraldry, part of a shield (3.07). (b) the lower part of a building, or of an architectural or ornamental feature, eg Attic base (1.05).

Base cruck (2.08): a type of cruck used as a roof support.

Basement (1.15): (a) the lowest storey in a house, frequently partly underground. (b) the lowest part of a building, or of an architectural or ornamental feature.

Base moulding (1.06): the first moulding above the plinth of a column or wall.

Basilica: in classical architecture, a large rectangular Roman hall with colonnades and a semi-circular apse, used primarily as a court of law. By the 4th century adapted as one of the basic plans for Christian churches in Western architecture, as opposed to the cruciform plan adopted in Constantinople for the East.

Basket weave bond (2.02): a standard bricklaying arrangement.

Bas-relief: sculptural decoration in low relief, in which none of the figures or motifs are separated from their background.

Bastion (1.07): a pentagonal work projecting from the main rampart. Dominant feature of European military architecture from the 16th to 19th centuries.

Bat (2.02): a cut brick.

Bathroom (1.15): a room for washing.

Baths (1.02): public bathing facilities, a centre of social life in ancient Rome.

Batter: a sloping wall.

Battlement (1.07): a parapet with rectangular indentations for use by the defenders of a fortified building. Since the 15th century also used for decoration.

Bauhaus: German school of architecture and design (1919–33) founded by the architect Walter Gropius. Epitomised the marriage of modern design, mass production, industrial design and a teutonic romantic approach to abstract art. Housed in Weimar until 1925 and at Dessau until 1932, it was finally closed down by the Nazis and during its diaspora ruled in an austere manner modern architecture and design until the 1970s.

Bay: (a) a type of window (2.14). (b) one of a series of uniform divisions of the nave or roof of a medieval building, particularly ecclesiastical.

Bay curved window (2.14): a type of window.

Bay leaf garland (3.04): a classical ornamental motif.

Bay window (2.14): see Bay and also Bay curved window.
Bead (3.03): an ornamental motif.
Bead butt: a type of thick, highly fire-resistant door panelling.
Bead and reel (3.02): a type of moulding.
Beaded (3.02): see Moulding.
Beaded mortar joint (2.02): a type of mortar joint.
Beak: see Moulding.
Beak-head : (a) decorative motif with a bird's head and protuberant beak common in the decoration of Norman architecture. (b) captured war galley's prow (rostrum) or decorative effigy with them (rostral column) in Roman, Renaissance and later times.
Beam (2.09): a horizontal timber.
Bearer: a horizontal load-bearing timber.
Bearing wall: a load-bearing wall.
Bear's head couped (3.05): an ornamental device.
Bed (2.02): the lower surface of a stone or brick.
Bedroom (1.13, 1.14, 1.15): a room for sleeping.
Beech: European and Asian hardwood commonly used in the construction industry.
Beehive house: small primitive prehistoric stone structures, they are still in use in Apulia (heel of Italy) and called 'Trulli'.
Behrens, Peter [1868–1940]: designer and architect who moved from the orbit of the Arts and Crafts Movement to design of factories, shops and industrial products in Germany. A father of modernism; Gropius, Mies van der Rohe and Le Corbusier all worked in his AEG design office (1910
Belfry/Bell-gable/Bell-turret/Bell-cote (1.08): the top room of a tower in which bells are hung. Or, alternatively, the bell tower itself.
Belgian truss (2.09): type of truss used as a roof support.
Bell: (a) hollow metal musical instrument that rings when struck, used particularly for the Christian call to prayer (1.08). (b) part of a capital (1.06).

Belvedere: Palazzo Guadagni, Florence 1506

Belvedere: an open-sided roofed terrace, usually at the top of a building, with a commanding or interesting view of town square, formal garden, or landscape.
Bema: (a) a speaker's platform in ancient Greece. (b) the raised area in Early Christian churches exclusively reserved for the clergy.
Bendy (3.08): a division of a heraldic field.
Bendy sinister (3.08): a division of a heraldic field.
Bernini, Gianlorenzo [1598–1680]: the Italian sculptor who dominated the history of Roman Baroque art. Also an architect of immense distinction, whose buildings (eg the Baldacchino in Saint Peter's 1624–33 and Palazzo di Montecitorio 1650 onwards) have in many ways determined the architectural character of Rome until today.
Beton brut: concrete textured by leaving the impress of the form in which it is moulded. Sometimes timber is used to create a grained surface effect.
Bevel: see Moulding.
Bevelled (3.08): a cut brick.
Bevelled board (2.04): a type of wood siding.
Bezantry (3.08): a division of a heraldic field
Billet (3.09): a type of moulding.
Birch: a very hard European hardwood commonly used for furniture, plywood and veneer.
Bitumen felt: an asphalt roofing material.
Blind storey also Blind window: see Triforium.
Blocking buttress (1.12): a type of buttress used in medieval church

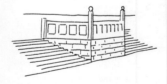

Bema: Athens Agora

©DIAGRAM

architecture.

Blocking course (1.12): a course of masonry above a cornice at the top of a building, especially classical.

Board and batten (2.03): a type of wood siding.

Board on board (2.04): a type of wood siding.

Boar rampant (3.05): an ornamental device.

Boar's head couped (3.05): an ornamental device.

Boast: stonework roughly fashioned with a boaster chisel prior to detailed carving.

Boiserie: French shallow relief wood carving and panelling.

Bolection moulding: a continous moulding of any decorative type that joins two surfaces at unequal levels.

Bolster/Corbel piece/Crown plate/Head tree/Saddle: a horizontal piece of timber at the top of a column or post to spread the bearing area under a beam.

Bolt lock (2.16): the part of a lock which actually prevents a door opening.

Bond (2.01, 2.02): a system of overlapping rows or courses of stones or bricks used to strengthen the construction of walls. There are a large variety of standard named patterns.

Bonding brick: a specially shaped brick used to hold together the two sides of a double-skinned wall.

Bordure (3.09): a heraldic charge.

Bordure embattled (3.09): a heraldic charge.

Borromini, Francesco [1599–1667]: the most original Roman Baroque architect, the rival of Bernini. His first great success was the tiny church of S. Carlo alle Quattro Fontane [1638–46] in which a truly original use of space triumphed over a very difficult and diminutive site.

Boss (2.07): an ornamented stone either at the end of an architectural feature, or more usually decorating the crossing points of the ribs of vaulted ceilings.

Bottom cripple (2.10): a part of a wood-framed structure.

Bottom panel (2.16): a lower panel in a door.

Bottom rail (2.16): the horizontal bottom part of a door.

Bouleuterion: a Hellenistic senate or council building.

Boullée, Etienne-Louis [1728–99]: very influential French classical architect whose emotional approach to design led to a style that was romantic in scale and feeling.

Bouleteurion: Miletus c170BC

Bow window: see Bay window.

Bowtell (3.01): see Round moulding.

Box frame: a type of construction in concrete suitable for buildings requiring repetitive rows of rooms such as apartments, hotels and prisons. The weight of the building is carried on cross-walls.

Box handle (2.16): a type of door handle.

Box stair: American term for an enclosed stairway.

Box window (2.14): a type of window frame.

Boxwood: a very strong hardwood.

Brace: (a) in carpentry any diagonal piece of timber placed in the angle formed by the two principal timbers. (b) a type of support used in roof construction (2.09).

Brace blocks: wooden keys used to secure beams.

Braced frame: in carpentry a type of wooden building frame.

Bracket (1.12): a weight-bearing support projecting from a wall or column. In medieval architecture usually referred to as a corbel; in classical architecture as a console.

Bramante, Donato [1444–1514]: leading Italian High Renaissance architect. Born near Urbino he was influenced by Alberti and Leonardo. His greatest work was in Milan and Rome where in 1506 he began the rebuilding of St Peter's on a Greek cross plan, only abandoned on the death of his patron Pope Julius II in 1513

Brasses (1.10): common term for sepulchral portrait monuments made in brass usually found on the floor of churches.

Brattices (1.07): wooden overhead screens for castle defenders.

Brattishing: the ornamented parapet of a wall.

Breakfast bar (1.15): in modern domestic architecture, a high counter in the kitchen for the informal eating of breakfast.

Breast/Chimney breast (2.08): the projecting area above a fireplace containing the hearth and flue.

Bressumer/Breastsummer: a very heavy beam either used across an opening such as that for a fireplace or shop window, or as a key timber in a timber-framed house.

Breuer, Marcel Lajos [1902–81]: Hungarian architect, studied and worked at the Bauhaus and later practised in the USA. He tempered a severe International Modern style with an instinctive feeling for raw materials.

Brick (2.02): standard building block made from clay burnt in a kiln. Different countries have varying basic shapes and specifications.

Brick construction (2.02): wall building with brick.

Brick core: a type of aggregate of filling made of brick behind the masonry on the front of an arch.

Brick nogging : the brickwork filling the areas between the pieces of a wooden-framed building.

Brickwork (2.02, 2.03): the art of building in brick.

Bridge: a structure carrying a road, railway or path across a natural or artificial obstacle.

Brindle brick (2.02): a brick with a striped surface.

Brise-soleil: a fixed shutter of horizontal slats used as a sunbreak above or across windows in hot climates.

Broach (1.08): pyramidal shapes formed by the placing of an octagonal spire over a square tower.

Broached (2.01): a type of stone dressing.

Broach spire (1.08): an octagonal spire surmounting a square tower in English medieval church architecture.

Broken course: an arrangement of masonry in modern stone walling.

Brown, Lancelot (Capability) [1716–83]: English Palladian country house architect most famous as the creator of the informal English landscape garden, as at Warwick Castle and Blenheim Palace.

Brunel, Isambard Kingdom [1806-59]: British Victorian engineer, designer of the Clifton Suspension Bridge, the Great Western Railway from London to Bristol, famous ships, such as *Great Western* and *Great Eastern* and the docks at Monkwearmouth, Bristol.

Brunelleschi, Filippo [1377–1446]: a Florentine, the first great architect of the Italian Renaissance was also a goldsmith and sculptor. His most famous architectural work was the dome and lantern which completed the building of the Duomo (cathedral) in Florence [1420–38].

Brutalism: term for uncompromisingly modern style of architecture which from the mid-1950s works on a huge scale in raw and exposed materials such as concrete.

Bucrane/Bucranium (3.05): a decorative motif on classical sculpture featuring the garlanded skull of an ox.

Bud (1.06): a type of capital.

Bulkhead: a rectangular-shaped cover for a water tank or other object

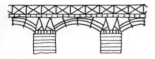

Bridge: Trajan's Danube Bridge AD104 by Apollodorus of Damascus

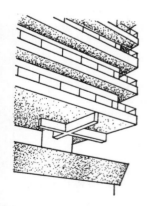

Brutalism: the Barbican Estate, City of London 1970 by Bon, Chamberlin and Powell

©DIAGRAM

on a concrete roof.

Bull (1.06): a type of capital.

Bull header (2.02): a standard position in brickwork.

Bull nose (2.16): a meeting profile of a door.

Bull stretcher (2.02): a standard position in brickwork.

Bungalow: Hindustani word for a single-storey domestic house first popularised by the British Raj.

Burlington, Richard Boyle, 3rd Earl of [1694–1753]: English patron and connoisseur of Palladian architecture. Also designed his own buildings such as Chiswick House (c1725), based on Palladio's Villa Rotonda.

Butterfield, William [1814–1900]: distinguished English Gothic Revival architect predominantly ecclesiastical. His adherence to the principles of Gothic art did not outweigh the originality of his use of shape and colour.

Butterfly wall tie (2.02): a type of metal tie.

Buttery (1.13): in medieval architecture, a storage room for food and drink.

Buttress (1.08): masonry support along the side of a wall. A flying buttress is a detached pier linked to a wall by an arch and thus supporting the weight and thrust from the vaulting of a roof rather than only that of the side wall.

Byzantine: Church of the Holy Apostles, Salonika c1320

Byzantine architecture (see style timechart): a style of Christian architecture, which developed after the establishment of the capital of the Roman Empire at Byzantium (Constantinople) by the Emperor Constantine in 330. Byzantine architecture and decoration initially created a synthesis of Hellenistic, Roman and Early Christian style. In the West it gave way to a Romanesque vernacular, in the Eastern Empire it developed until the fall of Constantinople in 1453, creating a type of centrally planned, highly decorated, domed church architecture which was exported to the Balkans, Russia and throughout the Middle East.

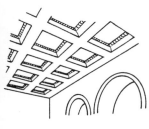

Caisson: roofing

Cable moulding (3.02): a type of spiral moulding.

Caisson/Coffer: (a) a recessed panel in a flat, vaulted or domed roof, which reduced weight and added a decorative element (2.06). (b) a watertight chamber used in the construction of foundations in modern architecture.

Caldarium/Calidarium (1.02): the hottest room in a Roman bath.

Calefactory: a room with a fire for cold monks in a medieval monastery.

Calk/Caulk/Tang: a steel bar used for strengthening masonry.

Callicrates [active 449–425BC]: the greatest architect of Periclean Athens and, with Ictinus, the builder of the Parthenon [447–432BC].

Caltrap (3.06): an ornamental device.

Calvary cross (3.09): a heraldic charge.

Camber arch (2.12): a type of segmental arch.

Campanile (1.08): Italian for a bell tower detached from the main body of a church.

Campen, Jacob van [1595–1667]: Dutch Palladian architect mainly in The Hague and Amsterdam who combined classical motif with Dutch brickwork and Dutch hipped roofs.

Canephorus: Athenian

Canadian spruce: whitish softwood used in joinery and for structural timbers.

Canephorus: female figure sculpture with basket on the head used as a column.

Canopy (2.16): a protective roof or hood over a door or window, or an object such as a tomb or a pulpit.

Cantilever: in modern engineering a projection such as a balcony which is self-supporting, eg without brackets, braces or columns.

Canton (3.09): a heraldic charge.

Cap (2.10): in joinery, part of a wood structure.

Capital (1.03, 1.06): the architectural feature at the head of a column.

Capping: see Coping.

Capstone: see Coping.

Carolingian architecture: style deriving from the court of the Emperor Charlemagne [768–814] in France, Germany and the Low Countries, reflecting his attempt to re-create a Roman Imperial style in the North, and looking forward to European Romanesque.

Carpenters Gothic: early Gothic Revival designs common in mid to late 18th century rustic woodwork.

Carport: in America a sheltered area for a motor car adjacent to a house with the same function as a garage.

Cartouche: a decorative ornamental tablet resembling a scroll of paper with the centre either left plain or with an inscription.

Caryatid (1.06): female sculpted figure used as a column, most famously in the porch of the Erechtheum in Athens.

Casemate: in military architecture a covered strongpoint loopholed for the defenders' small arms or artillery.

Casement window (2.15): a type of window.

Cast stone also reconstructed stone, also patent stone: imitation stone used as a replacement for masonry as a facing for buildings.

Castle (1.07): a fortified building, set of buildings, or place.

Catacomb: subterranean burial ground, best known as used by the early Christians outside the walls of Rome.

Cathedral: a Christian church which is also the seat of a bishop and hence the centre of an episcopal see.

Causeway (1.07): a raised pathway through water, hence part of medieval military defences.

Cavetto (3.01): a type of moulding.

Cavity/Hollow wall (1.12, 2.02): a double brick wall with a space of approximately 2in between each leaf, connected by wall ties. Common in Britain.

Ceiling: the overhead lining of a room either plastered, panelled, boarded or of stone or brick in medieval buildings.

Ceiling joist (2.10): in carpentry the joist on to which a ceiling is attached but which does not carry the floor above.

Cell: (a) a small room in a castle or a monastery. (b) one of the sub-divisions of a vault.

Cella (1.01): a store room in a Roman town house.

Cellar: in medieval building a regular store room, now used only when below ground level.

Cement: a binder used for making concrete or mortar out of aggregates.

Cemetery: burial ground; in Christian times usually attached to a church.

Cenotaph: a monument to those buried elsewhere.

Centering: the use of temporary wooden curved frame works during the construction of an arch or vault.

Chain: (3.04): a type of motif.

Chain lock (2.16): a type of door lock.

Chalet: a Swiss mountain hut.

Chamber: a room.

Chambers, Sir William [1723–96]: British Georgian architect, also a founder member of the Royal Academy. Rather academic but immensely successful in an English Palladian mould as at Somerset

Carolingian: Gatehouse, Lorsch Abbey, Germany c800

Cartouche: 16th to 18th centuries

Cenotaph: Whitehall, London 1920 by Lutyens

©DIAGRAM

House, London [1766–86].

Chamfered (3.01): a type of moulding.

Champfer (1.12): a 45° angle cut away from a masonry block or a piece of wood.

Chancel (1.09): the East end of a Christian church originally reserved for the clergy and containing the main altar and the choir. Loosely used to describe the whole area of a medieval church east of the crossing.

Chancel screen (1.09): the screen in a Christian church dividing the nave from the chancel.

Chantry (1.09): a small self-contained chapel, usually inside but sometimes outside a medieval church, financially endowed by the founder so that regular masses could be said for the repose of his soul.

Chapel: (a) a small church which is not a parish church. (b) a Nonconformist church. (c) a side altar in a discrete area within a church or cathedral (1.09).

Chapter-house (1.07, 1.09): the administrative meeting place of a monastery or cathedral.

Checky (3.08): a division of a heraldic field.

Cheneau: American term for the ornament on a cornice or gutter.

Chequer (2.01) : a wall built of two contrasting materials such as flint and stone or brick and stone, with a resulting chessboard effect decoration.

Chestnut: an easily workable timber which resembles oak and is used for fencing and gates.

Chevet (1.09): a type of east end of a medieval church in which the aisle continues behind the chancel with chapels radiating from it.

Chevron (3.03): a zig-zag ornamental motif.

Chevronny (3.08) a division of a heraldic field.

Chief (3.07): a part of a heraldic shield.

Chimney (1.13, 2.08): the structure in a building which encloses the flue or flues from a fireplace.

Chimney back: a thick wall behind a chimney.

Chimney bar: an iron bar above a fireplace which delimits and supports the chimney breast.

Chimney breast (2.08): a projecting wall in a room which houses the fireplace, hearth and flues.

Chimney can: see Chimney pot.

Chimney cowl (2.08): a revolving metal cover and ventilator above a chimney.

Chimney pot (2.08): a clay tubular pipe above a chimney stack to keep smoke clear of the stack.

Chimney shaft (2.08): free standing chimney.

Chimney stack (2.08): a collection of flues above roof level contained within a single masonry structure.

Chinoiserie: 18th century European interpretations of Chinese style in buildings such as pagodas. Most common on porcelain and in interior decoration.

Chisel: (a) a carpenter's cutting tool. (b) a type of pattern in wooden walling (2.04).

Choir (1.09): the area of a church used by the choir or by monastic community for singing their Office.

Choir-screen: a wooden screen dividing the choir from the nave of a church.

Church (1.08, 1.12): term for an ecclesiastical building used by any Christian denomination.

Churrigueresque (see style timechart): exuberant 18th century Spanish

Churrigueresque: Facade, Cathedral of Santiago de Compostela 1749 by Casas y Noboa

Baroque architectural style, epitomised by the three Churriguera brothers from Barcelona, incorporating elements of Latin American art and decoration.

Ciborium: see Baldacchino.

Cill: see Sill.

Cinquefoil (3.06): in tracery, a circle with five cusps.

Cinquefoil arch (2.13): cinquefoil tracery at the apex of a window.

Circular arch types (2.13): see Arch.

Circular stair (2.11): a spiral stair.

Circus: (a) a hippodrome for horse and chariot racing. (b) a circular arrangement of terraced houses, as in Bath, England.

Cistercian style: severe Romanesque architectural style used by the Cistercian order of monks founded at Citeaux (France) in 1098 and which rapidly spread throughout Europe.

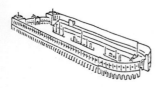

Circus: Circus Maximus, Rome cAD300

Citadel: a fortified place attached to, or within, a city.

Cladding/Siding (USA): the non-loadbearing covering of external walls.

Clapboard/Clapperboard: see Weatherboard.

Clapper bridge: crude bridge structure made of large slabs of stone.

Classical orders (1.04, 1.05): in Classical architecture the five standard arrangements and decorations of column, base, capital and entablature: Doric, Tuscan, Ionic, Corinthian and Composite.

Classical style (1.04, 1.05): a style of architecture and decoration, broadly based on ancient Greece and Rome (1.04, 1.05) which recurs constantly throughout the history of Western European art, particularly since the Renaissance up to the 19th century.

Clerestory/Clearstory (1.08, 2.09): mainly used in church architecture, for the upper rows of windows which are above the roofs of the side aisles; also the whole level of elevation containing such windows.

Clinker block/Cinder block (USA): cheap building block made of concrete.

Cloister (1.09): a covered area around the four sides of a square courtyard providing living and working space in medieval monastries.

Closer (2.02): part of a brick.

Closet: (a) a toilet or water closet. (b) in the USA any small room.

Cluny: the centre in Burgundy from 910 of an ascetic revival of Benedictine monasticism .

Clustered column (1.06): see Compound column.

Coade stone: an artificial cast stone popular for ornamental work in the 19th century.

Cockatrice (3.05): an ornamental device.

Cock bead (3.02): a type of moulding.

Coffering (2.06): see Caisson.

Collar (2.09): see Roof supports.

Collar beam gable (2.10): part of a wooden roof.

Collar-beam roof (2.09): a type of wooden roof.

Colonnade: a row of columns.

Column/Pillar/Pier/Shaft (1.03, 1.06): an upright circular support.

Combination window (2.15): a window frame which can be fitted with an extra layer of protection in stormy weather.

Comfort station (USA): WC and wash place.

Common/American bond (2.02): see American bond.

Common ashlar (2.01): see Ashlar.

Common/Floor/Boarding joist: wooden supporting boards spanning the area between walls, and on to which floor boards can be directly nailed.

Common brick/Building brick (USA): cheap local brick.

©DIAGRAM

Common rafter (2.10): sloping wooden support in roof construction.

Company (3.08): a division of a heraldic field.

Compartment: a sub-division of a building.

Compass/Radial/Radiating brick: tapering brick for circular walling.

Compass roof: a roof with curved rafters.

Compass window (1.11): a bay window.

Composite order (1.04): one of the derived orders of classical architecture.

Compound column (1.06): a column or pillar surrounded by a cluster of attached, or semi-detached shafts.

Concave mortar joint (2.02): a type of mortar joint.

Conch: a half dome in the apse or eastern end of a church.

Concrete: common binding agent in architecture since the pyramids and rediscovered by the Romans, a mixture of water, sand, stone and, in modern times, portland cement.

Confessio: an underground chapel for the burial of saints.

Conical broach (2.05): see Turret.

Conoid: of conical form.

Conservatory (1.15): glass greenhouse which can combine the function of growing and protecting plants and domestic use.

Console: a projecting bracket on a wall.

Continuous coil spiral (3.03): an ornamental motif.

Continuous ledger (2.09): part of a wood-framed structure.

Continuous stud (2.09): part of a wood-framed structure.

Conurbation: a group of towns that have grown into each other creating undisciplined urban sprawl.

Coping (2.01): a flat or sloping cover of stone or brick to protect the top of a wall.

Corbel (1.07, 1.12, 2.08): a block of stone projecting from a wall to support a beam or other weight.

Corbelled arch (2.13): a type of pointed arch.

Corbelling (2.05): rows of corbels carrying a wall proportionately farther outwards the higher it rises.

Corbie-steps: steps up the edge of a gable common in East Anglia and the Low Countries.

Cordon: a protected rampart.

Corinthian order (1.04, 1.05): third order of classical architecture.

Corner post (2.09): part of a wood-framed structure.

Cornice (1.03, 1.12, 2.09, 2.15): the upper and projecting part of an entablature in Classical architecture.

Corona (3.02): part of a cornice, see also moulding.

Corrugated iron (2.07): cheap galvanised corrugated steel sheeting for roofing.

Corrugated metal tie (2.02): a type of metal tie.

Cortile: an internal arcaded courtyard in an Italian building.

Cortona, Pietro Berrettini da [1596–1669]: Roman Baroque architect and painter, specially famous for his theatrical use of concave and convex shapes as in the church of S. Maria della Pace (Rome 1656–7).

Cottage: a small country dwelling place usually originally built for a farm labourer and his family.

Counter potent (3.07): a heraldic tincture.

Counterscarp (1.07): in military architecture, the side of a ditch nearest to the enemy.

Counter vair (3.07): a heraldic tincture.

Course: parallel layers of bricks, stones or wooden blocks in wall construction.

Cove/Coving: (3.01) a concave moulding used at the juncture of a wall and ceiling.

Covered way (1.07): (a) in military architecture, an infantry entrenched position all along the outer side of the main ditch. (b) an external roofed passageway.

Cowl: a metal rotating cover on a chimney.

Cramp-iron: a metal bar used to strengthen brickwork or masonry.

Credence/Credenza: a small table near the altar of a church to hold the bread and wine.

Crenellation (1.07): a defensive battlement or parapet with alternating lower areas for shooting purposes.

Crenelle: the higher part of a crenellation.

Crepidoma (1.01): the basic support of a Greek temple, with steps on all four sides.

Crescent: (a) a crescent-shaped row of terraced houses. (b) an ornamental device (3.06).

Crescent: Royal Crescent, Bath 1775 by John Wood the Younger

Crest/Cresting (2.08): an ornamental finish at the top of a wall or at the side of a roof.

Crested (3.08): a division line in heraldry.

Cretan and Mycenaean: the earliest architectural style of the Ancient Greek world destroyed in the 12th century BC. Mainly known from the excavations at Knossos and Phaestos on Crete.

Crocket (1.08): decorative foliage appearing on spires and pinnacles and canopies in Gothic architecture.

Cross: the symbol of Christianity.

Cross arellans (3.06): an ornamental device.

Cross botonée (3.06): an ornamental device.

Cross cramponée (3.06): an ornamental device.

Cross crosslet (3.06): an ornamental device.

Cross fimbriated (3.06): an ornamental device.

Cross fleurettée (3.06): an ornamental device.

Cross moline (3.06): an ornamental device.

Cross of Lorraine (3.06): an ornamental device.

Cross patée (3.06): an ornamental device.

Cross pommée (3.06): an ornamental device.

Cross potent (3.06): an ornamental device.

Cross recorcellée (3.06): a heraldic device.

Crossing: in a Christian church the area of intersection between the nave, chancel and transepts, usually underneath the tower.

Crown (2.12): part of an arch.

Crown post (2.09): an upright beam in a timber roof.

Crucks (2.09): arched pairs of timbers used in roof supports.

Crypt: the chapel or underground area beneath the nave of a church.

Cryptoporticus: an underground passageway.

Cubicula (1.01): bedroom in a Roman house.

Culina (1.01): the kitchen of a Roman house.

Cull (2.02): part of a brick.

Cult statue (1.01): object of veneration in a Classical temple.

Cuneus (1.02): wedged-shaped area of seating in a classical theatre.

Cupola (2.06): a dome.

Curtail step (2.11): the bottom step of a staircase.

Curtain wall: (a) a wall with towers surrounding a courtyard in medieval architecture (1.07). (b) a non-loadbearing wall in modern building.

Curvilinear tracery (1.11): a form of elaborate flowing tracery.

Cushion (1.06): a type of capital.

Cusp (1.11): a pointed element within a Gothic arch, or in Gothic tracery.

Cyclopean masonry: see Polygonal.

Cyma (3.01): an alternatively convex and concave moulding.

Cyma recta (3.01): a type of cyma moulding.

Cyma reversa (3.01): a type of cyma moulding.

Cymatium: the topmost part of a cornice.

Dado: (a) in classical architecture, the central part of a pedestal between the base and the cornice (2.09). (b) also the panelling or decorative border on the lower half of a room's walls, above the skirting board.

Dagger (1.11): a motif in tracery.

Dais: a raised platform at the end of a hall on which the family head, or dignitaries, dine.

Damp course: a layer of water-resistant material laid in a wall just above ground level to exclude water from penetrating a building.

Dance, George, the Younger [1741–1825]: English Neoclassical architect whose finest work was London's Newgate Prison (1769–78). His expressionistic use of classical motifs anticipated the work of Sir John Soane.

Dancetty (3.08): a division line in heraldry.

Dancetty floretty (3.08): a division line in heraldry.

Daubing: rough plasterwork.

Dead light (2.14): a glass window fixed directly to its frame and which does not open.

Decastyle (1.03): a classical portico with ten columns.

Decorated style (see timechart): the second distinct phase of English Gothic architecture, prevalent from the 1290s to the end of the 14th century. Simple geometrical forms, conventional yet fresh foliage, and the ogee arch are typical characteristics.

Decrescent (3.06): an ornamental device.

Delorme/De L'Orme, Philibert [1500/15–70]: French architect who studied at Rome 1533–6 and helped to introduce classical architecture to France.

Demi-column (1.06): half-column embedded in a wall.

Demi-lion (3.05): an ornamental device.

Dentil/Dentel (1.05, 3.02, 3.03): toothlike classical ornament used in cornices.

Depressed three-centred arch (2.12): a type of arch form.

Dexter (3.07): part of a heraldic shield.

Dexter base (3.07): part of a heraldic shield.

Dexter chief (3.07): part of a heraldic shield.

Dexter fess (3.07): part of a heraldic shield.

Diaconicon: see Vestry.

Diagonal bond (2.02): a standard bricklaying arrangement.

Diagonal brace (2.09): part of a wood-framed structure.

Diagonal buttress (1.12): a buttress at the corner or angle of a building.

Diagonal rib (2.06): a type of rib vaulting.

Diagonal wood flooring: a type of wooden flooring.

Diamond wood pattern (2.04): a pattern in woodwork.

Diaper work: the repetitive use of an ornamental motif to create a regular decorative pattern.

Diaphragm arch: a transverse arch dividing the wooden roof of churches into sections.

Diastyle (1.05): a system of columniation in which the intervals between columns are three times the column's diameter.

Diazoma (1.02): a semicircular passageway in the auditorium of a classical theatre.

Decorated style: Exeter
Cathedral, England c1365

Die (1.05): the central part of a pedestal, see also Dado.
Dimetric projection (3.10): a type of drawing projection.
Dining room (1.15): a room for eating.
Dipteral (1.03): a classical temple completely surrounded by a double row of columns.
Disappearing stair: a folding stair to a roof or loft.
Discharging arch: see Relieving arch.
Distyle (1.03): a classical portico with two columns.
Distyle in antis (1.03): columniation with alternating pairs of circular pillars and square pieces.
Ditch (1.07): a channel dug in the ground, for defensive or drainage purposes.
Division wall: a fire-resistant wall between houses.
Dodecastyle (1.03): a classical portico with 12 columns.
Dogleg staircase (2.11): a stair with no well and two flights between storeys.
Dog rampant (3.05): an ornamental heraldic device.
Dog tooth (3.03): an ornamental motif.
Dolphin (3.05): an ornamental device.
Dome (2.05): a hemispherical vault, ceiling or cupola.
Domed turret (2.05): a type of turret.
Domical vault (2.05): a dome divided into cells divided by groins.
Door (2.16, 2.17): a hinged, sliding or raised panel for closing the entrances to a building or a room.
Door knob (2.16): a handle on a door.
Doric order (1.04, 1.05): the first order of classical architecture and decoration.
Doric Roman (1.04): a Roman adaptation of the Doric order.
Dormer (2.14): an upright window projecting from a sloping roof.
Dormitory: a multi-occupancy sleeping room.
Double arched (3.08): a division line in heraldry.
Double cone (3.03): a type of moulding.
Double Flemish bond (2.03): a standard bricklaying arrangement.
Double glazing: double layer of window glass for protection against severe weather or traffic noise.
Double header (2.10): a part of a wood-framed structure.
Double hung window (2.15): a type of window.
Double-pitched roof (2.05): a type of roof.
Double return staircase (2.11): a type of stairway.
Double Roman tile: a standard British roofing tile.
Double slide door (2.17): a type of door.
Double swing door (2.17): a type of door.
Double tressure (3.09): a heraldic charge.
Double tressure flory (3.09): a heraldic charge.
Double trimmmer rafter (2.10): a part of a wood-framed structure.
Douglas fir: the most commonly used softwood by the building industry in Britain and the USA.
Dovetailed (3.08): a line division in heraldry.
Dowell: see Cramp-iron.
Downpipe/Downcorner/Rainwater pipe (2.08): a vertical pipe for draining water from a roof.
Dragon beam/piece (2.09): part of a wood-framed structure.
Dragon device (3.05): an ornamental device.
Drawbridge (1.07): a bridge over a moat or ditch, which can be pulled up in the face of the enemy to deny access to a fortress.

Early Christian: Mausoleum of Constantia (S. Constanza), Rome AD330

Early English: Westminster Abbey N Transept, London, 1260

Elizabethan: Hardwick Hall, Derbyshire 1597

Empire: Chamber of Deputies portico, Paris 1807 by Poyet

Dressed stone (2.01): stone used in masonry walling which has been squared and smoothed on its surface.

Dressings: (a) edgings for walls of better quality and more finished stone than the main surface. (b) types of finish for the surface of masonry (2.01).

Dripstone: a moulding above doors and windows to throw off rainwater.

Drop arch (2.13): a type of pointed arch.

Drum (2.06): the circular upright support for a dome.

Dry masonry (2.01): walling laid without mortar or cement.

Dry stone wall (2.01): a type of wall made without mortar.

Dummy breast (1.15): a chimney fireplace without outlet for smoke but for decoration only.

Duplex apartment: American term for a maisonette, a flat or apartment on more than one floor.

Dutch arch: see Flat arch.

Dutch bond (2.03): (a) English cross bond or (b) Flemish bond.

Dutch door (2.17): a stable door.

Dutch gable (2.18): an ornamental stepped gable at the top of a house front.

Dwarf gallery (1.08): a small arcaded passage on the outside of a building.

Eagle displayed (3.05): an ornamental device.

Early Christian architecture (see style timechart): Christian buildings exist for the 3rd century, in particular meeting houses, catacombs and martyria. From the conversion of Constantine (312) onwards, the Roman basilican form was adopted as the ground plan for church architecture until the development of centrally-planned Byzantine building.

Early English (see style timechart): the first style of English Gothic architecture, prevalent from the late 12th century to the late 13th century. Although French in origin, its ground plan, decoration and elevation are from the outset specifically English in style.

Easter sepulchre: a recess in the north chancel of a medieval church to hold the effigy of the risen Christ during Easter celebrations.

Eave/Eaves (2.05): the overhanging lower part of a roof.

Echal: the cupboard in a synagogue which contains the rolls of the Law.

Echinus (1.03): a type of moulding.

Edge bedded (2.01): a position of stones in masonry walling.

Egg and dart moulding (3.03): an ornamental motif.

Egg and tongue (3.03): an ornamental motif.

Elizabethan architecture (see style timechart): Early English Renaissance architecture during the reign of Elizabeth I (1558–1603) and a little after, see Tudor.

Elliptical arch (2.13): a type of circular arch.

Elm: a common hardwood.

Embattled (3.08): a division line in heraldry.

Embattled gaudy (3.08): a division line in heraldry.

Embrasure (1.07): opening in a crenellated parapet, also splayed parapet or wall opening for cannon.

Empire (see style timechart): decorative style common throughout Europe in the wake of Napoleon.

Enceinte (1.07): the main perimeter of a castle or fortified place.

End (2.02): a part of a brick.

End scroll (3.04): an ornamental motif.

Engaged column (1.06): a column which is not free-standing but is sunk into a wall or pier; see also applied column.

English bond (2.03): a standard bricklaying arrangement.
English cross bond/Saint Andrew's cross bond (2.03): a standard bricklaying arrangement.
English flooring (2.10): a type of flooring pattern.
English garden wall bond (2.03): a standard arrangement in bricklaying.
Enneastyle (1.03): a classical portico with nine columns.
Ensuite bathroom (1.15): a bathroom leading directly off a bedroom.
Entablature (1.03): the upper part of an order of architecture, or visual beam, comprising the cornice, frieze and architrave.
Entasis (103): the convex swelling in the middle of a classical column, designed to counteract the optical illusion of the outline being concave.
Ephebeum/Ephebeion (1.02): a room for gymnastics in classical public baths.
Epistylium: see Architrave.
Equilateral arch (2.13): a type of pointed arch.
Erminois (3.07): a heraldic tincture.
Escallop (3.05): an ornamental device.
Escarp: see Scarp.
Escartelly: a division line in heraldry.
Escutcheon: (a) in heraldry, a whole coat of arms (3.09), or, (b) the field on which the arms are painted. (c) a decorative surround to a keyhole.
Estipite: a pilaster that narrows towards its base.
Estoile (3.06): an ornamental device.
Etruscan architecture (see style timechart): building style of the Romans' predecessors in Italy. Only Etruscan city walls and elaborate tombs, rich in decoration, survive.
Eustyle (1.05): a system of columniation in which the intervals between columns are 2½ times the column's diameter.
Eyebrow (2.14): a type of roof window.
Exedra (1.01, 1.02): in classical buildings a recessed area, semicircular or rectangular, for discussions and disputations.
Expressionism (see style timechart): North European architectural style prevalent in the first quarter of the twentieth century that did not treat buildings as purely functional, but also as exciting sculptured objects in their own right, eg Gaudi in Spain, Klint in Denmark; Poelzig and Mendelsohn in Germany.
Extrados (2.12): the exterior curve of an arch.
Extruded mortar joint (2.02): a type of mortar joint.
Facade (1.03): the main front of a building.
Face (2.02): a part of a brick.
Face bedded (2.01): a position of stones in masonry walling.
Facing: the finishing, usually of brick, stone or plaster, covering the outside surface of a building.
Facing bond: a standard arrangement in bricklaying, showing mainly stretchers.
Face bricks (USA): decoratively coloured or textured bricks for use on the facing of a wall.
Fane: see Vane.
Fan light (2.16): a window over a door.
Fan tracery (2.07): specifically English style of late Gothic vaulting, fan-shaped and elaborately decorated with stone tracery.
Fan vault: see Fan tracery.
Fascia (3.01): a type of moulding.
Fasteners: metal screws, bolts and hooks for fastening woodwork.
Fauces (1.01): narrow passage in a Roman house, from the Latin for

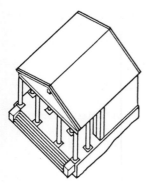

Etruscan: Temple of Apollo, Veii, Etruria 6th century BC

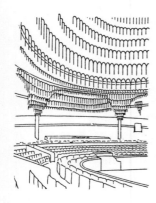

Expressionism: Great Playhouse, Berlin by Poelzig 1919

©DIAGRAM

jaws.

Fenestration: the window arrangement on any building.

Ferro-concrete: see reinforced concrete.

Fess (3.07): part of a heraldic shield.

Festoon/Swag: a carved ornament of fruit and flowers. Also in banding form (3.04).

Fillet (3.01): a simple flat band that separates mouldings.

Finial (2.08): carved ornamental foliage on top of a pinnacle, spire, gable or canopy.

Fireback: the wall, or cast iron plate, at the back of grate.

Firebrick: a fire-resistant brick.

Fireplace (1.13, 1.15): open space in a room, under a chimney, for a fire, hearth and grate.

Firestopping: (a) thick timber to act as a firebrake in a wooden structure (2.10). (b) a layer of fire-resistant blocks in a brick wall.

Fir trees eradicated (3.05): an ornamental device.

Fischer, Johann Michael [1692–1766]: South German Rococo architect who built 22 abbeys and 32 churches all richly decorated, frequently monumental and spatially subtle.

Fischer von Ehrlach, Johann Bernhard [1656–1723]: Austrian Baroque architect who rose to become Imperial Court Architect (1704). His Saltzburg churches, Prague and Vienna palaces constitute an impressive reminder of the grandiose but harmonious Habsburg Baroque style he evolved. Best known of all are the Schönnbrunn Palace (1696–1711), the Karlskirke (begun 1716), and the Hofbibliothek (1723, finished by his son Joseph). His *A Plan of Civil and Historical Architecture* (1721) was the first to analyse Chinese and Egyptian architecture.

Fish hauriant (3.05): an ornamental device.

Fishscale (2.04): a pattern in woodwork.

Fivefold cross (3.06): a heraldic device.

Flamboyant: Church of St Maclou West Front, Rouen 1514

Flamboyant (see style timechart): late French Gothic style, distinguished by sinuous wavy tracery.

Flasques (3.09): a heraldic charge.

Flat/Apartment (USA): a single storey unit of habitation in a multi-storey building.

Flat/Straight/French/Jack arch (2.13): a type of arch. Jack arch is the US term.

Flat frieze (1.05): a plain frieze.

Flat pratt truss (2.09): a type of modern truss used as a roof support.

Flat roof (2.05): a roof which is horizontal and does not slope.

Flat warren (2.09): a type of modern truss used as a roof support.

Flaunches (3.09): a heraldic charge.

Flèche: (a) (1.08) a very small wooden spire. (b) in military architecture, a small v-shaped outwork.

Flemish bond (2.03): a standard bricklaying arrangement since the 17th century.

Flemish diagonal bond (2.03): a standard bricklaying arrangement.

Flemish double header bond (2.03): a standard bricklaying arrangement.

Flemish garden wall bond (2.03): a standard bricklaying arrangement.

Flemish spiral bond (2.03): a standard bricklaying arrangement.

Fleuron: as finials

Fleur-de-lis (3.06): an ornamental device.

Fleuron: a flower-shaped ornament.

Flight (2.11): a series of stairs joining one floor to the next, or one floor to a landing.

Flint wall: a wall made of flints.

Floor joist (2.10): a part of a wood-framed structure.
Florentine arch (2.13): a type of circular arch.
Flower, four-leaved: ornamental flower with four leaves.
Flush bead moulding (3.02): a type of moulding.
Flush door (2.17): a type of door.
Flush work (1.12): the use of knapped flint and dresser stone to make patterns.
Fluted column (1.06): a column with a fluted shaft.
Fluted torus (3.02): a type of moulding.
Fluting (1.06): a form of observation consisting of shallow, vertical concave grooves.
Fluting banding (3.03): an ornamental motif.
Flying/Monk/American bond: a standard bricklaying arrangement.
Flying buttress: see Buttress.
Foils (1.11): the foil is the space between a cusp within a circle or arch, decorated as foliage or as a feather. Quatrefoil and trefoil are multiple arrangements.
Folding door (2.17): a type of door.
Folding window (2.17): a type of window.
Foliated: the use of leaf-shaped foils as ornament.
Foliated capital (1.06): a type of capital decorated with foliage.
Folly: a sham building, sometimes a ruin, built to enhance a vista or a landscape.
Font: a large raised fixed basin in a church containing holy water and used for baptism.
Fontana, Carlo [1638–1714]: Rome-based architect who worked for ten years under Bernini and influenced pupils throughout Europe such as Pöppelmann (Germany), Gibbs (England), Fischer von Ehrlach and Hildebrandt (Austria).
Footing: (a) a wall foundation (1.12). (b) a type of stone edging on a masonry wall (2.01).
Forked cross (3.06): an ornamental device.
Formy fitchy cross (3.09): a heraldic charge.
Forum: Roman term for Agora, an open space surrounded by public buildings.

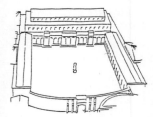

Forum: Trajan's Forum, Rome, AD117 by Apollodorus of Damascus

Foster, Sir Norman : [b1935] current British architect working in the so-called high-tech style with designs in East Anglia (E England) and Hong Kong (HK and Shanghai Bank HQ 1986).
Four-centred (Tudor) arch (2.13): a type of pointed arch.
Fourchée cross (3.06): an ornamental device.
Framed building: a building supported by a frame (timber, steel or reinforced concrete) rather than by load-bearing walls.
Frame house: a method of wooden house construction.
French casement/door/window (2.17): a type of door.
Fret: (a) an ornamental motif (3.03). (b) a division line in heraldry (3.09).
Fretty (3.09): a heraldic charge.
Frieze: (a) the middle section of an entablature (1.03). (b) an ornamental band, either abstract, botanical or figurative around the upper walls of a room below the cornice.
Frigidarium (1.02): the cool room in a Roman bath.
Frithstool (Freedstool): in some medieval churches a stone seat near the altar for those seeking sanctuary or refuge within the church.
Frog (2.02): part of a brick.
Front door (1.13, 1.15): main entrance door in a house.
Full cruck (2.09): a type of roof support.

Frieze: from Triple Archway, Hyde Park Corner, London c1825 by Decimus Burton

©DIAGRAM

Functionalism (see style timechart): a building created by an architect who emphasises the functional aspects of the design, without any decoration, symbolism or apparent aesthetic consideration. Eventually, this leads to a style that expresses the building's practical purpose rather than abstract aesthetic considerations.

Fusil (3.09): a heraldic charge.

Fusily (3.08): a division of a heraldic field.

Fylfot (3.06): an ornamental device.

Gable (2.05, 2.08): the triangular, or sometimes semi-circular, top of a wall which supports and provides ends to a pitched roof.

Gabled dormer (2.14): dormer window with a gabled end.

Gabled roof (2.05): a type of roof with a gabled end.

Gable end stud (2.10): part of a wood-framed structure.

Gablet: (a) a small decoration on the theme of a gable (2.05). (b) sometimes used for a gabled dormer (2.14).

Gaboon: a hardwood, a type of African mahogany.

Gabriel, Ange-Jacques [1698–1782]: French Neoclassical architect who in 1742 became Premier Architect to Louis XV and Madame de Pompadour. His works were elegant and refined, avoiding the excesses of Rococo, and were imbued with good taste and beautiful proportions. Among his masterpieces are the Petit Trianon palace at Versailles (1762–8) and the Place de la Concorde, Paris (1755).

Gadroon (3.03): an ornamental motif with convex curves.

Galilee (1.09): a porch or chapel sometimes attached to the west end of a church or cathedral.

Gallery: in ecclesiastical architecture, the upper storey over the aisle, and below the triforium and clerestory.

Gambrel/Half-hipped roof (2.05): a type of roof.

Garage (1.15): room or separate building for housing motor vehicle(s).

Garage door: a door that interconnects between a house and its garage.

Garb (3.05): an ornamental device.

Garden-wall bonds: see American bond and Flemish bond.

Garderobe (1.07): a medieval lavatory.

Gargoyle (1.08, 1.10): a spout carrying water off a roof, and frequently decorated with grotesque heads.

Garnier, Tony [1869–1948]: visionary early modern French architect who designed a Cité Industrielle that heralded a new approach to town planning. He built a slaughterhouse and stadium (1909–16) at Lyons, both featuring his love of reinforced concrete and cantilevers.

Garreting : splinters of stone inserted into the joints of coarse masonry, such as flint walls.

Gatehouse (1.07): the rooms, or apartments, above a fortified medieval medical gateway.

Gaudi, Antoni y Cornet [1852–1926]: Catalan Spanish architect, the most famous and extreme builder and designer in Art Nouveau style. His best known work, the Cathedral of the Holy Family in Barcelona, was begun in 1883 and remains incomplete – in part due to the impossibility of reconciling an almost Baroque and very three-dimensional design with the realities of architecture.

Gauged arch: an arch made from gauged bricks.

Gauged brick: a type of brick.

Gazebo: a small summerhouse or pavilion with a view, or a belvedere on the roof of a house.

Geometrical staircase (2.11): a type of staircase.

Geometrical tracery (1.11): a tracery form.

Georgian (see style timechart): term loosely used (and much

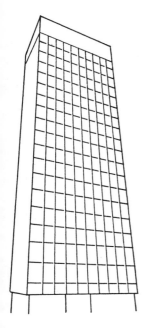

Functionalism: Seagram Building, New York 1958 by Mies van der Rohe and Johnson

Gazebo: nr Würzburg, Germany, 18th century, by Antonio Petrini

Georgian: Stoneleigh Abbey, Warwickshire, England 1726 by Francis Smith

subdivided) to describe English Late Renaissance classical architecture during the reigns of the four Georges (1714–1830).

Giant/Colossal order : an order of columns that rises through more than one storey without any interrupting capitals or entablature.

Gibbs, James [1682–1754]: a Catholic Scottish architect who studied in Rome and mastered the Italian Mannerist and Baroque styles. His most famous building is the Church of St Martin's-in-the Fields, London (1722–6), his most original the Radcliffe Camera theatre, Oxford (1737–49) and his *Book of Architecture* (1728) may have prompted the White House, Washington.

Gothic: Notre Dame Cathedral, Paris 1325

Gibbs surround: a heavy masonry decoration surrounding a window or doorway, made up of alternating long and short masonry blocks.

Gilly, Friedrich [1772–1800]: short-lived Prussian architect whose highly original, bold and functional designs' use of the classical style make him a precursor of modern architecture.

Giulio, Romano [1492/9–1546]: Roman Mannerist painter and architect whose most famous work was at the court of Federigo Gonzaga in Mantua, especially the Palazzo del Te (1525/6–31).

Glacis (1.07): the slope from the top of a fortified parapet to the open countryside on the outside, giving complete fire coverage to the defenders.

Glass door (2.17): a type of door.

Glazing bar (2.14): a part of a window.

Golden section: a semi-mystical proportion,(actually measuring 1:1.618) known to the Greeks and enthusiatically developed in the Italian Renaissance and by Le Corbuiser for his Modular (see entry).

Gothic Revival: Manchester Town Hall, England, 1877 by Alfred Waterhouse

Goss bridging (2.10): a part of a wood-framed structure.

Gothic (see style timechart): predominant European style of architecture from the 12th to the 15th centuries characterised by the use of the pointed arch, the rib vault and the flying buttress. It is a style most noted for its church architecture in which the religious aims are height and light, both achieved through a mixture of skeletal structures, ever increasing windows, vaulting and the transference of weight downwards and sideways via rib and buttress.

Gothic Revival (see style timechart): historicist, romantic and catholic attempt to revive medieval Gothic architecture and ornament from the late 18th to the end of the 19th centuries. It ranged from the picturesque love of ruins and Gothic follies, to the state symbolism of the Houses of Parliament in London (1834) and the high seriousness of Victorian ecclesiastical building.

Greek architecture: unfinished Temple at Segesta, Sicily c416BC

Goutty (3.08): a division of a heraldic field.

Grape banding (3.03): an ornamental motif.

Greek architecture: the classical period of Greek architecture lasted from the 7th to the 4th centuries BC. The zenith was reached with the Parthenon at Athens (c449–444BC) which exemplified a formal, proportional, trabeated architectural style that has established an endlessly self-perpetuating canon of taste into the late 20th century.

Greek cross: (a) the Byzantine cross, with the four arms of equal length. (b) an ornamental device (3.06). (c) the layout of a Byzantine centrally-planned church (1.09).

Greek Revival: The British Museum, London 1847 by Sir Robert Smirke

Greek Revival (see style timechart): the specifically Greek contribution to Neoclassical architecture only became known about 1750. Such knowledge inspired Ledoux, Soane and a host of Victorian followers. At its best the Greek Revival stood for a purity and simplicity of structure and form.

Griffin (3.05): an ornamental device.

Grotesque: Worcester
Cathedral, England

Grille: an ornamental arrangement of metal bars to form a screen or partition.

Groin (2.07): the curved area formed by the intersection of two vaults.

Gropius, Walter [1883–1969]: German Bauhaus architect who became the grand old man of modern architecture's International Style from his training under Peter Behrens, through his foundation of the Bauhaus, to his postwar work at Harvard, USA.

Grotesque: exotic flora and fauna in ornamental motif, adapted from the Romans who had used them in dank and underground buildings.

Ground floor (1.15): the floor of a building on ground level.

Guarini, Guarino [1624–83]: leading Italian Baroque architect and mathematician, all of whose surviving buildings are in Turin, eg the Capella della SS Sindone (1667–90).

Guest bedroom (1.15): extra bedroom for those who come to stay.

Guilloche (3.04): an ornamental motif based on a variety of interlaced circles and wavy bands.

Gules (3.07): heraldic term for the colour red.

Guttae (1.05, 3.03): moulded ornament with cone-shaped drops, originally in a Doric entablature.

Guttering (2.08): a channel along the edge of a roof to drain away water.

Gymnasium: classical Greek centre for physical training.

Gyron (3.09): a heraldic charge.

Gyronny (3.08): a division of a heraldic field.

Half moon (1.07): see Ravelin.

Hall (1.13, 1.15): large room in a house or dwelling place; used as living room in a medieval house and an entrance area in a modern one.

Hall church : a type of church common in Germany in which the aisles are the same height as the nave, which is therefore lit from the aisle windows.

Hallway (1.15): a longitudinal entrance hall or corridor.

Hammerbeam (2.09): a type of roof truss.

Hand rail (2.11): a rail alongside a stairway at hand height.

Hanging door (2.17): a type of door.

Hanging style (2.14, 2.16): see Window.

Hardouin-Mansart, Jules [1646–1708]: highly successful French Baroque architect to the court of Louis XIV. From 1678 he was in charge of the development of Versailles. His contributions to Paris include the Place Vendôme (1698) and the Invalides Chapel (1680–91).

Hardwood: wood, mostly hard in texture as well as name, from broad-leaved deciduous trees.

Harmonic proportions: classical Greek theories, repeated in the Renaissance especially by Alberti and Palladio, relating the proportions of music to those of architectural design.

Haunch (2.12): a part of an arch.

Hawksmoor, Nicholas [1661–1736]: a highly original English Baroque architect who worked for, and with, both Wren and Vanbrugh. His own genius is best seen in his six City of London churches such as Christchurch, Spitalfields (1723–39).

Header: (a) a position in brickwork (2.02). (b) part of a window (2.14). (c) part of a door (2.16).

Hellenistic: the development of Greek architecture from the 4th to the 1st centuries BC in the kingdoms existing (323–30BC) after the death of Alexander the Great.

Helm roof (1.08): a type of roof.

Heneage knot (3.06): an ornamental device.

Henostyle (1.03): a classical portico with only one pillar.

Hellenistic: Mausoleum (el-Khazna), Petra, Jordan 1st century BC

© DIAGRAM

71

Heptastyle (1.03): a classical portico with seven pillars.
Herringbone: an ornamental motif (3.04) in brickwork (2.03), masonry or cabinet-making.
Herse: a portcullis.
Hexastyle (1.03): a classical portico type of columniation with six pillars.
Hickory: North American timber used for tool handles.
Hildebrandt, Johann Lucas von [1668–1745]: Austrian military engineer and Baroque architect whose Vienna and South German palaces were even more Italianate (à la Guarini) than Fischer von Ehrlach's. Prince Eugene's Belvedere summer palace (1714–24) is his masterpiece, containing characteristic octagonal and oval rooms off spectacular staircases.
Hinge (2.16): a fixture for hanging a door.
Hip flashing (2.08): a roof finish along its edge to prevent water leaking through.
Hip-knob: a pinnacle or finial on the hips of a roof, or at the apex of a gable.
Hipped dormer (2.14): a type of window.
Hipped gabled roof (2.05): a type of roof.
Hipped roof (2.05): a type of roof.
Hip roof (2.05): a type of roof.
Hollow moulding (3.01): a type of moulding.
Hollow wall: see Cavity wall.
Holy water stone/stock/stoup (1.10): stone basin, sometimes on a pillar, near the entrance to a church containing holy water.
Honduras mahogany: a Central American wood.
Hood (2.14): see Window.
Hood mould (1.12): a projecting moulding above an arch or a window.
Hopper window (2.15): a type of window.
Horse rampant (3.05): an ornamental device.
Horseshoe arch (2.13): a type of circular arch.
Hôtel: a large French town house.
Hourdes (1.07): see Brattices.
Hungarian flooring (2.10): a type of flooring pattern.
Hyperbolic paraboloid roof: a roof in the form of a double-curved shell.
Hypocaust: the chambers or ducts in a Roman underground central heating system.
Hypogeum: any underground part of an ancient building.
Hyposkenion (1.02): a part of a classical theatre.
Hypostyle: a thickly pillared hall, especially in ancient Egypt, in which the roof rests directly on the columns.
Hypotrachelion (1.05): a groove on a Doric column between the capital and the shaft.
Iconostasis: in a Byzantine church, the screen between the nave and the chancel.
Ictinus (active c447–430BC): the most important architect of Periclean Athens, and hence one of the known founders of Western architecture. With Callicrates he built the Parthenon (447–432BC).
Imhotep (active c2980/2630–2950/2611BC): Old Kingdom 3rd Dynasty Egyptian architect and the first recorded by history. Designed Pharaoh Djoser's Step Pyramid at Saqqara. Probably fhe only architect to be deified.
Imperial (2.05): see Turret.
Impluvium (1.01): the basin in the centre of an atrium in a Roman house, used to catch the rainwater from the central opening (compluvium).

©DIAGRAM

Impost (2.12): a part of an arch.
Increscent (3.06): an ornamental device.
Indented (3.08): a division line in heraldry.
Inescutcheon (3.09): a heraldic device.
Inglenook: a corner by a chimney.
Inner bailey (1.07): central area of a medieval fortress.
Intarsia: an inlay or mosaic made up of different coloured woods, common in Renaissance Italy.
Intercolumniation (1.05): classical system of spacing between columns, as measured in diameters.
Interlocked roof (2.07): a type of roof.

International Modern: Harvard Graduate Centre, Cambridge, Mass 1950 by Gropius

International/International Modern Style (see timechart): the rational style in 20th century architecture, as pioneered by architects like Frank Lloyd Wright and Walter Gropius, spread by the Bauhaus, and at its most influential in the 1930s.
Intersecting tracery (1.11): a form of window tracery.
Intrados (2.11): a soffit, an element in an arch.
Invected (3.08): a division line in heraldry.
Ionic order (1.04): the second order of classical architecture.
Irregular coursed (2.01): an arrangement of masonry in modern stonewalling.
Isidore of Miletus [active 532–7]: Byzantine architect and geometrician who assisted Anthemius of Tralles in building Hagia Sophia at Constantinople.

Islamic architecture: Dome of the Rock, Jerusalem AD691

Islamic architecture: the early architecture of Islam incorporated much existing Christian building. This changed with the Dome of the Rock in Jerusalem (685–91). Minarets were first built in the 8th century. Fully developed urban and decorative Islamic building, using brick, tile and stucco, became more independent of Byzantium and the Hellenistic and subsequently spread as far afield as Spain and West Africa to Central Asia, India and Indonesia.
Isometric projection (3.10): a type of drawing projection.
Jacobean (see style timechart): architectural style named after James I (1603–25) that incorporates the first precise rendering of Italian Renaissance style and motif in British architecture.
Jacobsen, Arne [1902–71]: Danish International Modern architect (also a furniture and jewellery designer) who used the rationalism of the 1930s with a constant precision and elegance as seen in Denmark's private houses and town halls.
Jamb: the side pieces of windows (2.14) and doors (2.16).

Jacobean: Charlton House, Kent 1612 by Adam Newton

Jefferson, Thomas [1743–1826]: third president of the USA and influential architect in large part responsible for a stylistic mixture of Serlio, Palladio and Gibbs that dominated American neoclassical architecture, especially in the new capital city of Washington and Jefferson's own Virginia home, Monticello.
Jerkin head roof: see Hipped gable.
Jesse window: stained glass window in a medieval church's east (altar) end depicting Christ's genealogy as a Tree of Jesse.
Jib/Gib door: a door flush with a wall to render it as inconspicuous as possibe.
Johnson, Philip Cortelyou [b1906]: American architect who coined the term International Modern and was originally one of its most famous protagonists, as in the New York Theater at the Lincoln Center (1962–4). He later became a founding father of post-Modernism.
Jointing: joining brickwork or masonry with mortar while it is still fresh, rather than by pointing.

Joint: the mortar between brickwork or masonry.
Joist: see Ceiling joist.
Jones, Inigo [1573–1652]: English Renaissance painter, architect and designer of costume masques. His buildings, such as the Queen's House, Greenwich (1616–35) and the Banqueting House, Whitehall, London (1619–22), show an original interpretation of Palladio – Jones' designs for the theatre were more like exotic Italian baroque.
Jubé: see Rood screen.
Keel moulding (3.02): a type of moulding.
Keep (1.07): the central building of a medieval castle.
Kent, William [1685–1748]: English classical architect, painter, furniture designer and landscape gardener who, under the patronage of Lord Burlington, combined creatively a knowledge of Italian Baroque (he spent 10 years in Rome), Palladio, Vitruvius and Inigo Jones. His most famous building is Holkham Hall, Norfolk (1734).
Kentish rag: a rough limestone found in Kent and used as external mason
Key banding (3.03): an ornamental motif.
Keystone (2.12): the central element of an arch.
King closer (2.03): a part of a brick.
King post (2.09): a type of roof truss.
Kiosk: (a) a small pavilion or summer-house. (b) a small shop building on the street or inside a bigger building.
Kitchen (1.13, 1.15): a room for preparing and cooking food.
Knapped flint: a wall made of flints broken down the middle.
Kneeler (1.12): a stone at the top of a brick or stone wall.
Label (3.09): a heraldic device.
Label stop (1.12): an ornamented boss at the end of a hood moulding.
Laced windows (1.12): in early 18th century English architecture, a brick decoration in strips around a window to emphasise its shape.
Lacunar: the coffers in a panelled ceiling.
Ladder (1.13, 1.15): portable staircase or steps.
Lady chapel (1.09): a chapel at the east end of a medieval church, dedicated to the Virgin Mary.
Lancet arch (2.13): a type of pointed arch:
Lancet window (1.11): a type of window.
Landing (1.15, 2.11): platform joining two flights of stairs.
Lantern (2.06): a circular or polygonal structure above a dome, or roof for admitting light.
Lantern cross: a cross above a lantern.
Larch: a strong resinous softwood.
Larder (1.15): a room for storing food.
Latin cross (3.06): a type of cross.
Latrina (1.01): the lavatory of a classical or medieval house.
Latrobe, Benjamin Henry [1764–1820]: first American architect of international standing, born in England and trained there and in Germany. Emigrated to USA (1796) where he introduced both the Greek and Gothic Revival styles. Best known for his 1803–17 work on the Washington Capitol and White House, but his masterpiece is Baltimore Cathedral (1805–18).
Lattice window (2.15): a small window or light.
Laundry room (1.15): a room for washing clothes.
Lavatory: see Garderobe, Latrina, Privy, Toilet.
Leaded lights: small windows or lights set in lead surrounds.
Leaded window (2.15): a type of window.
Lean-to roof (2.05): a type of roof.
Le Corbusier (Charles-Édouard Jeanneret) [1887–1965]: Swiss-born

© DIAGRAM

French modern architect of unrivalled brilliance, influence and output. His early career as a cubist painter was reflected in his 1920s simple, almost cubist white private houses. The rationalism of International Modernism was apparent in his concern with city planning and with the mass production of housing. His later work, however, became anti-rationalist and sculptural such as the Chapel of Notre Dame at Ronchamp, France (1950–4). See Modulor.

Lectern (1.10): a desk or stand in a church to hold a bible or large service book.

Ledge and brace door (2.17): a type of door.

Ledoux, Claude-Nicolas [1736–1806]: a highly imaginative and original French neoclassical architect, with geometrical simplicity and an almost expressionist use of form, typified by his saltworks at Arc-et-Senans (1775–9). His career was ruined by the French Revolution and thereafter he only published the designs which have made him more highly considered in the 20th century than in his own lifetime.

Left hand door (2.15): a type of door opening configuration.

Left hand reverse door (2.15): a type of door opening configuration.

Leopard's face (3.05): an ornamental device.

Lesbian cymatium: see Cyma reversa.

Lesene : a pilaster strip used in Anglo-Saxon and Romanesque architecture to strengthen thin rubble walls.

Le Vau, Louis [1612–70]: the leading Baroque architect in France who, together with an integrated team of artists and decorators, created the Louis XIV style at Versailles.

Library (1.02): a room for storing and reading books.

Lierne (2.07): a rib used in vaulting.

Light (1.11): a part of a window.

Linenfold (3.03): an ornamental motif.

Lintel (2.16): a horizontal beam or bar across the top of a door, window or other opening.

Lion couchant (3.05): an ornamental device.

Lion coward (3.05): an ornamental device.

Lion passant (3.05): an ornamental device.

Lion queue fourchée (3.05): an ornamental device.

Lion rampant (3.05): an ornamental device.

Lion rampant guardant (3.05): an ornamental device.

Lion sejant (3.05): an ornamental device.

Lion sejant rampant (3.05): an ornamental device.

Lion's face (3.05): an ornamental device.

Lion's head (3.05): an ornamental device.

Lion's paw couped (3.05): an ornamental device.

Lion statant (3.05): an ornamental device.

Lissitsky, Eleazar Markevich [1890–1941]: Russian Constructivist architect, painter, typographer, designer and theorist. His concept of Proun involved the interaction of painting and sculpture. Worked in the West from 1922 to 1931 and influenced De Stijl.

Lock rail (2.15): a part of a door.

Loft (1.13, 1.15): a room immediately under the roof of a house.

Loft dormitory (1.13): a loft used for sleeping accommodation.

Loft door (1.15): a trap door to a loft.

Log framing (2.04): a type of wooden wall construction.

Logeion (1.02): speaking place of a classical theatre.

Loggia: an open-sided gallery, usually with pillars, common in Renaissance Italy.

London stock see Stock brick.

Loggia: Loggia dei Lanzi Florence, 1382 by Cione e Francesco

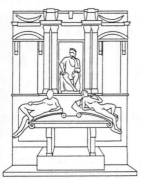

Mannerism: Monument to Lorenzo de Medici, Medici Chapel, Florence, 1534 by Michelangelo

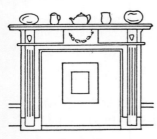

Mantelpiece: in Italian marbles by Adam 1758–92

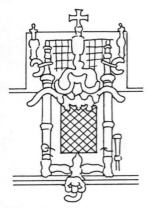

Manueline style: Window, Convent-Castle of Christ, Tomar after 1500

Mascaron: classical mask from Pompeii

Long and short work (1.12): the alternating of vertical and horizontal pieces of masonry to strengthen a wall or corner of a wall.

Lotus banding (3.04): a type of bandwork.

Lotus column (1.06): a type of column.

Lounge/Living room (1.15): a room for general daytime use.

Louvered door (2.17): a type of door.

Louvred window (2.15): a type of window.

Louvres: (a) a window opening made of overlapping boards to ventilate without letting in the rain (2.15). (b) a similar opening in the roof to let smoke escape from the hearth of a medieval hall.

Lozenge: (a) a type of motif (3.04). (b) a heraldic device (3.09).

Lozengy (3.08): a division of a heraldic field.

Lunette: (a) a semicircular opening. (b) in military architecture a separate triangular fortification on or outside the glacis or (c) a small fortification alongside a ravelin.

Lych gate: a covered wooden gate at the entrance to a churchyard.

Machicolation (1.07): opening between a projecting parapet's corbels for the defenders to pour boiling oil or other missiles down on attackers without being exposed to them. Replaced the earlier system of brattices.

Mackintosh, Charles Rennie [1868–1928]: leading Scottish architect of the Glasgow School whose Art Nouveau design integrated all aspects of building, decoration and furniture; especially at the School of Art (Library Wing), Glasgow (1907–9).

Mahogany: a common name for many hardwoods used in the building and cabinet-making trades.

Maltese cross (3.06): a type of cross.

Mannerism (see style timechart): the predominant style of Italian, and Italianate, architecture from Michelangelo to the end of the 16th century. A reaction against High Renaissance classical perfection, Mannerist architecture responded either with a frigid, rigorous application of classical rule and motif, or with the deliberate flouting of classical convention – ie by the misuse of motif and the juxtaposition of unlikely shape, scale and motif as in Michelangelo's Medici Chapel, Florence (1520).

Manor house: a medium-sized medieval house in the country or a village, the centre of a manor.

Mansard (2.05): a type of roof.

Mansart, François [1598–1666]: first great French classical architect, whose genius was early demonstrated in the Orléans wing of the Château of Blois (1635–8). His erratic nature, however, prevented many of his buildings from being completed. Brought the mansard roof into common use.

Manse: a house attached to a church and provided for the minister in Scotland and the English North Country.

Mantelpiece: a shelf above a fire place, usually integrated with the mantel, or fire surround.

Manueline style (see timechart): Portuguese architecture during and just after the prosperous reign of King Manuel I the Fortunate (1495–1521), the culmination of the late Gothic style.

Martello tower: English artillery coastal fortification copied from a tower captured in Corsica 1794; 74 were built on the east and south coasts of England against the French invasion threat 1805–12.

Martlet (3.05): an ornamental device.

Martyrium: a Christian church sited over the grave(s) of martyr(s) or one of the places in Jerusalem associated with Christ's Passion.

Mascaron: a grotesque head used in ornament.

Mausoleum: Mausoleum
of King Mausolas,
Halicarnassus, SW Asia
Minor, 351BC by Pythius and
Satyrus

Mascle (3.09): a heraldic device.
Masonry (2.01): the craft of stonework and stone walling.
Masonry stoop (2.16): a part of the steps to a doorway.
Master bedroom (1.15): main bedroom of a house, usually occupied by the owners or the most important inhabitant.
Mausoleum: a large, grand tomb comprising a separate structure or building.
Mendelsohn, Erich [1887–1953]: pioneer German Expressionist architect whose extreme use of streamlined curves was only achieved once in the Einstein Tower, Potsdam (1919–20). Although retaining an expressionistic look in his building, Mendelsohn's later work in Germany, England, Israel (hospitals) and the USA was sobered by 1930s International Modernism.
Merlon (1.07): the upright part in a crenellated battlement.
Mermaid (3.05): an ornamental device.
Metope (1.03): part of a frieze in the Doric order.
Metropolis: a capital or major city.
Meurtrière: narrow opening in a fortified wall for the firing of projectiles.
Mews: a small terrace of stables and staff accommodation in a cobbled street behind a row of rich town (especially London) houses.
Mezzanine/Entresol: in a multi-storey building, a small floor between the major floors, usually placed to one side.
Michelangelo Buonarotti [1475–1564]: Italian Renaissance sculptor, architect, painter and poet, his genius overturned all the classical theories, preoccupations, structural considerations and decorative motifs of the Early Renaissance. He sculpted rather than built his buildings, using mass, weight and decorative motif to create an organic and dynamic whole. He worked mainly in Florence, especially the Medici Chapel (1520–34) and the Library of San Lorenzo (the Bibliotheca Laurentiana 1524–6); and in Rome, especially the finishing of St Peter's (1546–64). Michelangelo not only created Mannerist architecture but also influenced, for better or worse, nearly all subsequent classical styles.
Middle base (3.07): part of a heraldic shield.
Middle chief (3.07): part of a heraldic shield.
Middle cruck (2.09): a type of roof support.
Middle panel (2.16): part of a door.
Mies van der Rohe, Ludwig [1886–1969]: German modern architect who moved swiftly from a neoclassical to an ultra-Expressionist style. Later, as director of the Bauhaus from 1930, became a pillar of International Modernism. His enormously influential role continued as head of the Illinois Institute of Technology in Chicago, for whom he designed a new campus (1939). His modernism remained unswervingly rational and wedded to the rigid integrity of the 1930s.
Mihrab: niche in a mosque indicating Mecca's direction.
Minaret: Islamic tower for calling the faithful to prayer at a mosque.
Minbar: a pulpit in a mosque.
Minster: a loose term given to a number of medieval English cathedrals and major churches. It originally implied a monastery and monastic church.
Minute: a unit of measurement in classical architecture and design based on 1/60th of a column's diameter.
Misericord (1.10): a support, often decorated and sculpted, on the underside of a winged seat in a choir stall, to help the monk or canon when standing at office or service.

Motte-and-Bailey: Norman, British Isles 1066–c1180

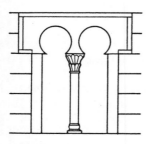

Mozarabic: Ajimez twin window, Church of San Miguel de Escalada, Leon, Spain 913

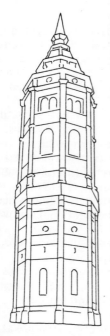

Mudéjar: Octagonal belfry tower of S Andres, Calatayud, Aragon 14th century

Moat (1.07): a defensive ditch full of water around a castle, fortress, town, or fortified manor house.

Modillion (1.05, 2.07): bracket supporting the upper part of a Composite or Corinthian cornice.

Modular design: modern design for mass production broadly based on the standard dimensions of prefabricated building parts. As a concept it was given philosophical respectability by Le Corbusier's theory of the Modulor.

Module: any unit of measurement which can be used to determine the proportions of buildings or parts of them. Hence a minute in classical architecture, modular design and Corbusier's modulor in modern architecture.

Modulor: proportional system used by Le Corbusier (see entry) and published in 1951. As in his Marseilles flats, the *Unité d'habitation* (1947–52), he used the male figure to create a scale for determining the proportional size of the parts of the building (a device not unknown to Leonardo da Vinci, and derived from the Golden Section).

Monastery: a building complex, including a church or abbey, inhabited by monks or nuns.

Monitor roof (2.05): a type of roof.

Monk/Yorkshire/Flying bond: a standard bricklaying arrangement modifying Flemish bond.

Morris, William [1834–96]: English designer whose Arts and Craft Movement influenced every aspect of architectural and interior design in the early modern period. His insistence on craftsmanship's integrity provided the intellectual justification for rejecting slavish copying of the past, yet his parallel rejection of machinery and mass-production's potential was inconsistent in some ways both with his social and cultural message.

Mortar: mixed binding material for laying bricks and masonry. Now almost universally a mixture of Portland cement, lime putty and sand.

Mortice and tenon: a right-angled joint in joinery.

Mosaic flooring: (a) a floor covered with mosaic decoration. (b) a pattern used in wooden flooring (2.10).

Mosque: a Muslim place of prayer and worship.

Motte: a hill or artificial mound around which many early English medieval castles were constructed.

Motte-and-bailey: a motte enclosed by a ditch and palisade and surmounted by a wooden (later stone) tower. Earliest example of this primitive castle form is on the River Loire (France) and is dated 1010.

Mouchette (1.11): a form in tracery.

Moulding (2.10, 3.01, 3.02): shaped decorative outlines on projecting cornices and members in wood and stone.

Mozarabic (see style timechart): Christian architecture and design in Iberia from the 9th to the 11th centuries which demonstrates the influence of Moorish and Islamic building style, especially the horseshoe arch (2.13).

Mudéjar (see style timechart): Christian architecture in Spain that was entirely Muslim in style, as opposed to Mozarabic which only borrowed a number of features and elements.

Mull (2.15): see Window.

Mullet (3.06): an ornamental device.

Mullet pierced (3.06): an ornamental device.

Mullion (1.11, 2.14): a part of a window.

Muntin: (a) a part of a door (2.16). (b) also see mullion (2.14).

Murrey (3.07): heraldic term for a mulberry-red colour.

Mutule (1.05): a part of a Doric cornice.

Nailhead (3.02): a type of moulding.

Naos: (a) the central room or sanctuary of a Greek temple (1.01). (b) the central area, or sanctuary, of a Byzantine centrally-planned church.

Narthex: (a) in a Byzantine church a room at the west end before the nave and aisles. (b) in western medieval church architecture a room or chamber added to the west end before entering the main body of the church (1.09).

Nash, John [1752–1835]: versatile and highly successful English Regency architect who used every known style from classical to Gothic to oriental exotic (Brighton Pavilion 1815) with equal fluency. His layout and building of Regent Street and Regent's Park, London (1811–28) combined delicate stucco facades and lightness of decorative touch with an heroic scale of town planning.

Natural bedded (2.01): a position of stones in masonry walling.

Nave (1.09): the main body of a church to the west of the choir, basicallly to accommodate the congregation. It usually has aisles on either side.

Nebule: see Nebuly.

Nebuly: (a) a division line in heraldry (3.08). (b) a type of moulding.

Necking (1.05, 1.06): part of a column capital.

Needle spire (1.08): a type of spire.

Neoclassical (see style timechart): late 18th century classical movement based on both a rational approach to design and movement, as opposed to Rococo exuberance, and a more correct archaeological interpretation of Greco-Roman architecture. Neoclassical architecture at its extreme (Soane in Britain, Latrobe in the USA, Zakharov in Russia and Ledoux in France) was almost abstract in the use of volumetric space – of the balance of simple shapes and mass; but for the most part it produced restrained, intelligent and humane classical designs.

Nervi, Pier Luigi [1891–1979]: Italian engineer, architect and inspired designer in concrete. Built stadia, aircraft hangars, exhibition halls and skyscrapers all with a mixture of elegance and technological daring, the hallmark of postwar Italian modern architecture. Famous examples are the Pirelli Building at Milan (with Gio Ponti 1955–8) and the Palazzo dello Sport (Rome, 1960).

Neumann, (Johann) Bathalsar [1687–1753]: the finest and most versatile German Rococo architect began as a military engineer. His creations, the Würzburg Prince Bishop's Residenz (1719–44) with its splendid formal staircase and about 100 churches, often oval-based in plan and sumptuously decorated, are the apotheosis of this mobile and decorative style.

New towns: 32 totally new urban environments created in Britain since 1946 with a population of over 2 million. English examples are Harlow and Milton Keynes. Most are more interesting as experiments in sociology and urban planning than as essays in architectural excellence.

Newel/Nowel/Nuel (2.11): part of a wooden staircase.

Niche (1.12): a recess in a wall or pillar to hold a statue or an object of worship.

Niemeyer, Oscar [b1907]: Brazilian modern architect who worked during 1936 in Rio with Le Corbusier. He developed his own anti-rational, expansive, sculptural style in the Church of St Francis at Pampulha (1942–3). He was chief architect for the creation of the new capital city of Brasilia (1957 onwards), full of breathtaking buildings, aesthetic contradictions, and severe practical and sociological problems.

Nogging (2.04): brickwork infilling of a timber-framed house.

Neoclassical: The United States Capitol, Washington DC 1867

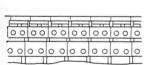

New towns: Runcorn New Town housing, Cheshire 1976 by Stirling

Norman: White Tower c1097 by William I & II, Tower of London

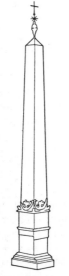

Obelisk: Egyptian obelisk St Peter's Square, Rome

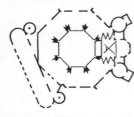

Octagon: Church of San Vitale, Ravenna, Italy 547

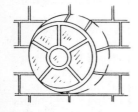

Oeuil-de-boeuf (Bull's eye)

Nombril (3.07): part of a heraldic shield.

Nookshaft (2.07): a small shaft in the angle of a pier.

Norman (see style timechart): the English name for Romanesque architecture, the first example of which was King Edward the Confessor's Westminster Abbey (1065), and which was further seriously imported from Normandy by William the Conqueror the following year. See also Romanesque.

Norman brick: a standard brick common in the USA.

Nosing (2.11): part of a staircase.

Nowy (3.08): a division line in heraldry.

Nursery (1.15): a room for small children.

Oak: the most famous English hardwood used as a structural timber.

Oak trees on mount (3.05): an ornamental device.

Obelisk: a monument of Ancient Egyptian origins, consisting of a tall tapering shaft of stone with a pyramidal top.

Oblong vault (2.07): a type of vault.

Oblique perspective (3.10): a method of perspective drawing and construction.

Octagon: an eight-sided polygon, the ground plan for usually small decorative buildings in the classical tradition.

Octagonal column (1.06): an eight-sided column.

Octastyle (1.03): a portico with eight columns.

Oculus (2.05): the opening (eye) at the apex of a dome.

Oecus (1.01): a main hall in a Roman house.

Oeillet: small circular loophole in medieval fortified wall for bows or guns to be fired from.

Oeuil-de-boeuf: an oval window.

Off-set: a horizontal ledge in a wall that reduces in thickness as it gets higher.

Ogee arch (2.13): a type of pointed arch.

Ogee moulding (3.02): a type of moulding.

Ogee roof (2.05): a type of roof.

Onion dome (2.06): a type of dome.

Opisthodomos (1.01): rear hall in a Greek temple, often used as a treasury.

Opus Alexandrinum: a type of ornamental mosaic paving.

Opus incertum (2.01): Roman walling with irregular stone.

Opus listatum: Roman walling with alternating brick and masonry courses.

Opus quadratum (2.01): Roman walling with square masonry.

Opus reticulatum (2.01): Roman walling with diagonally arranged squares of masonry.

Opus sectile: paving or walling covered with ornamental cut piece of soft marble.

Opus testaceum (2.01): Roman masonry in horizontal strips.

Or (3.07): heraldic term for the colour gold.

Orangery: a conservatory for growing oranges, glazed on the south side.

Oratory: a small private chapel.

Orders (1.04): the basic orders of classical architecture, perfected in ancient Greece, adopted and adapted by the Romans and the Renaissance, were Doric, Ionic, Corinthian and Composite. These ornamental treatments of the fundamentals of horizontal-beam architecture established canons of taste that still pertain in the post-Modernist world of the 1990s.

Oriel (2.14): a type of window.

Orientation: in Christian architecture, the siting of a church on an

©DIAGRAM

eastenwest axis, with the altar at the east end. This is extremely common, but there are important exceptions (eg St Peter's, Rome).

Orle (3.09): a heraldic charge.

Ottoman: generic term for Turkish Islamic architecture from the late 14th to early 20th centuries, under the rule of the 38 Ottoman sultans in SE Europe (Balkans), North Africa, Anatolia and the Middle East.

Ottonian (see style timechart): transitional period in German architecture between Carolingian and Romanesque.

Oubliette: a deep medieval dungeon where the prisoners were deposited through a trap door and forgotten.

Oud, Jacobus Johannes Pieter [1890–1963]: Dutch architect and member of De Stijl, a movement which stood for a severe cubistic approach to building, as opposed to the expressionistic. Specialised in public housing and estates, especially at Rotterdam (1918–27) and the Hook of Holland (1924–7).

Outer bailey/ward (1.07): an area in a medieval castle outside the inner walls.

Outer curtain wall (1.07): exterior defensive wall – outside the inner walls – of a medieval fortress.

Outhouse: a small building detached from a house, such as a garden shed or sometimes a privy.

Overdoor: see Sopraporta.

Ovolo (3.01): a type of moulding.

Pagoda: Buddhist Indian, SE Asian or Chinese temple in the form of a tower, copied as a decorative building in Europe from the 18th century.

P'ai Lou: a highly decorated Chinese gateway.

Palisade: a defensive fence of strong wooden stakes.

Palladianism (see style timechart): widespread classical style of architecture throughout Europe and the American colonies in the 17th and particularly the 18th centuries. Derived from the buildings and treatises of Andrea Palladio.

Palladio, Andrea [1508–80]: Venetian architect and theorist whose all-pervasive influence created the style internationally known as Palladianism. Studied the Roman architect Vitruvius, and was fascinated by Roman symmetrical planning and laws of harmonic proportions. He was also the Mannerist product of the art of his close predecessors such as Bramante, Raphael and Michelangelo. His villas, such as the Villa Rotonda, Vicenza (begun 1550) were the inspiration for much early 18th century English country house building.

Palm (1.06): a type of capital.

Palmette: decorative device based on a palm leaf.

Paly (3.08): a division of a heraldic field.

Paly bendy (3.08): a division of a heraldic field.

Pane (2.14): a section of glass in a window.

Panel door (2.17): a type of door.

Panelling (2.04, 2.10): the lining of a room's wall with a wainscot, a decorative wooden panel.

Panel tracery (1.11): a type of tracery.

Pantile (2.08): a type of roofing tile.

Pantry (1.13, 1.15): a small room for keeping food and cooking utensils.

Papal cross (3.06): a type of cross.

Papyrus (3.04) an ornamental motif.

Parabolic arch (2.13): a type of circular arch.

Parallel bevel (2.16): a meeting profile of a door.

Parapet: (a) a low wall at the edge of a large drop. (b) a protective wall in military architecture (1.07).

Ottonian: Palatine Chapel of Valkhof (Falcon's Court), Nijmeguen, Holland 10th century

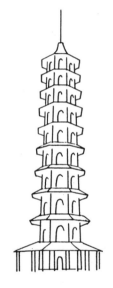

Pagoda: Kew Gardens, London 1761 by Chambers

Palladianism: Mereworth Castle, Kent 1730 by Colin Campbell

Parakklesion (1.09): a chapel in a Byzantine church.

Parclose screen: in a medieval church, a screen around a small altar or shrine.

Pargetting (2.04): the exterior plaster work on a timber framed building.

Parodos (1.02): gangway to the stage in a classical theatre.

Parquet (2.00); wooden flooring made of small symmetrically arranged pieces of hardwood.

Parted/Fretty cross (3.09): a heraldic charge.

Parterre: in garden design, a level area with ornamented flower beds close to the main house.

Parthenon: see Adyton.

Parvis: see Paradise.

Passage (1.13): an interconnecting area or corridor.

Pastrophory (1.09) : a room in an Early Christian or Byzantine church, usually off the apse.

Patera: a circular or oval ornament in clerical architecture.

Patriarchal cross (3.06): a type of cross.

Pavilion: a small light building such as a summer house.

Paxton, Sir Joseph [1801–65]: originally a gardener, he made greenhouses for the Duke of Devonshire at Chatsworth (1826–40). He designed and built the Crystal Palace (1851) for the Great Exhibition in London, important not only for its use of glass and metal, but also for its construction in prefabricated elements, the first major building of this nature.

Pean (3.07): a heraldic tincture.

Peardrop (3.03): an ornamental motif.

Pebbledash: see Roughcast.

Pedestal (1.05): the supporting parts of a column.

Pediment: (a) a low pitched triangular gable above a temple facade (1.03). (b) a smaller version of same above a door or window.

Penastyle (1.03): a portico with five columns.

Pendant (2.12): a part of a vaulted arch.

Pendentive (2.06, 2.07): a supporting part of a dome.

Penthouse: (a) an outhouse with a lean-to roof. (b) a separate structure on the roof of a high rise building.

Penthouse roof (2.05): a type of roof.

Pepperpot sentry box (1.07): conical, often ornamented enclosure at a bastion angle for soldiers to keep watch from under cover.

Per bend (3.08): a division of a heraldic field.

Per bend sinister (3.08): a division of a heraldic field.

Per chevron (3.08): a division of a heraldic field.

Per cross (3.08): a division of a heraldic field.

Per fess (3.08): a division of a heraldic field.

Per fess base per pale (3.08): a division of a heraldic field.

Pergola: a covered walk for growing plants over in a garden.

Peripteral (1.03): a building entirely surrounded by a single row of columns.

Peristylium/Peristyle (1.01): an open courtyard surrounded by columns.

Per pale (3.08): a division of a heraldic field.

Per pale and barry (3.08): a division of a heraldic field.

Per pale sinister half per fess (3.08): a division of a heraldic field.

Perpendicular (see style timechart) : the third and most English, of England's three Gothic architecture styles. Characterised by an emphasis on horizontals and verticals, by large windows, by lierne vaults and then fan vaults, it was common from the 1350s until the 16th

Perpendicular: West Front, Winchester Cathedral 1367–1404

©DIAGRAM

century, and in some areas, even later. It reached its height with buildings such as King's College Chapel, Cambridge (1446–1515).

Perret, Auguste [1874–1954]: French modern architect who was first in France consistently to use a concrete structure with its members deliberately exposed and integrated with the decorative design. Early examples, such as flats in Paris' Rue Franklin (1902–3), combined concrete construction with Art Nouveau detailing. Later, his work, such as the rebuilding of Le Havre (1946 onwards) was almost classical in its balance and austerity.

Perron: an external flight of steps leading to an exterior landing and an entrance to a church or the first floor of a house.

Per saltire (3.08): a division of a heraldic field.

Perspective drawing: the art of rendering three dimensions in a two-dimensional drawing. It played an essential part in Renaissance art theory.

Pew (1.10): wooden seating for the congreagtion in a church.

Pharos: a Greco-Roman lighthouse.

Piano nobile: the most important, usually the first, floor of a house, with rooms that are larger, grander and usually higher than the remainder.

Piazza: (a) a public outdoor space surrounded by buildings. (b) in English classical architecture, also a loggia.

Pier: (a) see compass column (2.06). (b) a masonry support in solid and not columnar form (1.12).

Pilaster (1.06): a part pier or column that is embedded in a flat wall from which it projects slightly.

Pillar: any upright supporting structure.

Pilotis: a building carried on pillars leaving the ground floor open.

Pinnacle (1.08): a south turret or tall pyramidal ornament used in Gothic architecture to surmount buttresses, parapets and other features high on church buildings.

Piscina (1.12): a stone basin with a drain near the altar in a medieval church for washing the sacred vessels.

Pitched roof: see Gabled roof (2.05).

Pivoting window (2.15): a type of window.

Plain tile (2.08): a simple roofing style.

Plaisance: a summerhouse in the grounds of a country mansion.

Plaster: a surface covering for wall and ceilings, applied wet, dries to smooth hard protective surface.

Plate tracery (1.11): a type of tracery.

Plateresque (see style timechart): the main architectural style of 16th century Spain, which mixed in an extravagant manner Gothic, Moorish and Renaissance decorative motifs. The term refers to silversmiths' work.

Plateresque: Palace gateway, Avila, Old Castile 16th century

Plinth: the base of (a) a wall (1.08, 2.10) or (b) a column pedestal (1.05).

Plinth block (2.16) : the piece at the bottom of the architrave of a door or chimney which corresponds to the skirting of the wall.

Podium (1.05): a continuous plinth supporting a row of columns.

Pointed cross (3.06): a type of cross.

Pointed horseshoe arch (2.13): a type of arch.

Pointed Saracenic arch (2.13): a type of arch.

Pointed segmental arch (2.13): a type of arch.

Pointed stone dressing (2.01): a method of preparing masonry.

Pointed trefoil arch (2.13): a type of arch.

Pointed trifoliated arch (2.13): a type of arch.

Pointing: mortar used to bind brickwork or masonry.

©DIAGRAM

Portico: Tate Gallery, London
1897 by S R J Smith

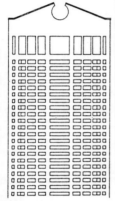

Post-Modernism:
'Chippendale chair
skyscraper at AT&T HQ, New
York 1983 by Philip Johnson
and John Burgee

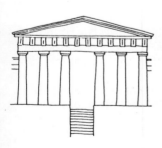

Propylaeum: to the Acropolis,
Athens 432BC by Mnesicles

Polygonal masonry (2.01): a stone walling arrangement.

Pöppelmann, Matthaeus Daniel [1662–1736]: German Baroque architect appointed to the Elector of Saxony's court (1705). His most original building was the partially-finished Zwinger pavilion or 'Roman arena' (his own description) at Dresden (1711–12).

Poppyhead: a finial carved with foliage and animals at the top of a choir stall, bench or pew.

Porch (1.08, 1.09, 2.16): an external construction protecting the entrance to a building.

Portcullis (1.07): an iron lattice gate that can be lowered to protect the entrance to a castle.

Porte-cochère: a large porch which a coach can enter.

Portico (1.03): a porch with columns and pediment; *prostyle* if it projects from a building, *in antis* if it is enclosed within a building.

Portland cement: the most common type of cement (patented 1824), so called because its colour resembles Portland stone.

Portland stone: a highly-resistant limestone from Portland in Southern England, much used for facing buildings in London.

Post: a main vertical support of a building.

Post and lintel: see Trabeated.

Postern gate (2.07): a small gateway at the side or back of a fortress, monastery or town wall.

Post-Modernism (see style timechart): 1970s reaction against International Modern Style's austerity and the commercialisation of modern structural techniques. Basically it reintroduced ornament and decorative motif to building, often in garish colours and illogical juxtaposition.

Potent (3.07): a heraldic tincture.

Potenty (3.08): a division line in heraldry.

Pre-fabrication: buildings in which substantial components, such as roof, floors or walls, are manufactured whole or in sections off the building site.

Presbytery: (a) the area of a church reserved for the high altar (1.09). (b) in the Catholic church, a priest's house. (c) in the Presbyterian church a local church court and congregation.

Prestressed concrete: see Concrete.

Privy (1.13): a lavatory, frequently an outhouse.

Profile: see Moulding.

Projected window (2.15): a type of window.

Pronaos (1.01): the portico or vestibule of a classical temple.

Propylaeum: a gateway complex to an enclosed temple area.

Proscenium: in a classical theatre, the whole area of the stage.

Prostyle (1.03): see Portico.

Prothesis: (a) see Credence. (b) in a Byzantine church a separate room for the preparation and storage of the Eucharist.

Pseudo-dipteral (1.03): a temple designed like a dipteral (1.03), but with one row of columns omitted on the sides.

Pseudo three-centred (2.13): a type of pointed arch.

Pseudo four-centred (2.13): a type of pointed arch.

Pseudo-peripteral (1.03): a temple without a pteroma, ie with the columns attached to the temple walls.

Pteroma (1.03): the space between the side walls of a temple and the colonndade.

Pteron (1.03): an external colonnade, especially in a Greek temple.

Pugin, Augustus Welby [1812-52]: English architect and designer and passionate promulgator of the Gothic Revival. His conversion to

©DIAGRAM

Catholicism gave him a religious rationale for the superiority of Gothic, but he also understood the structure, form and function of Gothic building and not just its picturesque qualities. He had few rich important commissions except for the Houses of Parliament (1839-52), London, for which he designed all the decorative elements to transform Sir Charles Barry's basic structure.

Pulpit (1.10): an elevated platform in a church for preaching and reading the lessons. See Ambo.

Pulvinated frieze (1.05): a convex frieze.

Purbeck marble: a fine limestone from Purbeck in Dorset, England, with a marble-like appearance.

Purlin (2.09): horizontal roof support.

Purpure (3.07): heraldic term for the colour purple.

Push plate (2.16): a piece of door furniture, for pushing the door open without marking the wood or paintwork.

Put-log hole: a put-log is a wooden moveable beam to support scaffolding; and a put-log hole is in the wall to support such a beam.

Pycnostyle (1.05): a system of columniation in which the intervals between columns are 1½ times the column's diameter.

Pylon: massive rectangular wedge-shaped structure flanking the gateway of an ancient Egyptian temple.

Pyramid: an Old or Middle Kingdom Egyptian royal tomb of pyramidal shape.

Pyramid: Great Pyramid of Cheops (Khufu), Giza, Egypt, Old Kingdom c2560BC

Quadrangle: a wide rectangular enclosure surrounded by buildings, especially a university college.

Quadrate cross (3.06): a type of cross.

Quadratura: illusionistic painting of the walls and ceilings of buildings.

Quadriga (1.03): a sculptured group of a four-horse chariot and driver as on the Brandenburg Gate, Berlin.

Quarry/Quarrel (1.11): a diamond-shaped window pane or shape in tracery.

Quarry faced: see Rustication.

Quarter pierced cross (3.09): a heraldic charge.

Quarter turn (2.11): a type of staircase.

Quarter winding (2.11): a type of staircase.

Quatrefoil (1.11, 3.06): see Foil.

Queen closer (2.02): part of a brick.

Queen post (2.09): a type of truss used as a roof support.

Quirk: see Moulding.

Quirk bead : see Moulding.

Quoin (2.01): cornerstones at the angles of buildings, usually laid alternatively one short and one long.

Rabbet/Rebate (2.16): meeting profile of a door.

Radburn planning: town planning which involves the complete separation of traffic from pedestrians.

Radiating chapels: chapels around the east end of a church.

Rafter (2.09): a roof support member.

Ragstone/Rag work (2.01): a masonry pattern in stone walling.

Raguly (3.08): a line division in heraldry.

Rainbow roof (2.05): a type of roof.

Raised cruck (2.09): a type of roof support.

Rampant arch (2.13): a type of pointed arch.

Rampart (1.07): a defensive wall or battlement.

Random coursed (2.01): an arrangement of masonry in modern stonewalling.

Raphael (Raffaello Sanzio) [1483–1520]: consummate High Renaissance

Rayonnant: Rose window,
North Transept, Notre Dame
Cathedral, Paris 1258

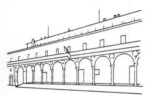

Renaissance: Foundling
Hospital, Florence 1444 by
Brunelleschi

Respond: Propylaeum
cAD249, Temples at Baalbek,
Lebanon

Rococo: Pilgrimage Church of
Vierzehnheiligen, Germany
1772 by Neumann

painter and architect. His building style took over from Bramante's late work. It is seen to best effect as much in his paintings, like *The School of Athens* (Vatican c1509), as in his actual building such as his last, the Chigi Chapel in S Maria del Popolo, Rome (c1513–14).

Rat-trap (2.03): a standard bricklaying arrangement.

Ravelin: triangular-shaped outwork fortification before the main curtain wall and generally placed between two bastions. Called *demi-lune*, ie half moon, in French.

Rayonnant (see style timechart): French mid-Gothic style relying on massive round stained-glass windows and a wholesale use of tracery.

Rayonny (3.08): a division line in heraldry.

Redwood: a common European and Asian softwood.

Reed and tie (3.02): a type of moulding.

Reeded torus (3.02): a type of moulding.

Reeding (3.03): an ornamental motif.

Reel (3.03): an ornamental motif.

Refectory: a communal dining hall.

Regula (1.04): a band within a Doric entablature.

Relieving/Rough/Discharging arch: an arch sprung clear of a weaker support in order to bear most of the weight.

Renaissance (see style timechart): in the broadest architectural sense, the Renaissance was a period in Italy from the 1420s to the mid-16th century within which the motifs and principles of ancient classical architecture were re-applied and integrated with the Italian architectural traditions. Italian Renaissance architects started with Brunelleschi and ended with Bramante, Raphael and Michelangelo. Italian Renaissance architecture, both in terms of theory, rule book and motif, was exported to the rest of Europe during the 16th century.

Reredos (1.10): a decorated screen behind an altar.

Respond: a half-pier or pillar at the end of an arcade.

Reverse ogee (3.02): a type of moulding.

Revolving door (2.17): a type of door.

Rib (2.07): a decorative and/or structural device which breaks up and emphasises the cells of a vault.

Ribbon (2.10): a board in wooden construction.

Ridge (2.05): the horizontal member at the apex of a pitched roof.

Ridge board (2.10): part of a wooden house structure.

Ridge rib (2.07): a type of rib in a vault.

Ridge tile (2.08): a type of tile.

Right hand (2.16): a door configuration.

Right hand reverse (2.16): a door configuration.

Rinceau : a decorative foliage motif.

Rise (2.12): the height of an arch.

Riser (2.11): a step in a staircase.

Rococo (see style timechart): a decorative anti-rational style of architecture that was at once the child and antithesis of the Baroque. In France it was associated with lightness, swirling forms and the frippery of the court; in South Germany and Austria with almost ecstatic exuberance and spatial complexity. It denied structure and dwelt on line and emotion, in buildings such as Balthasar Neumann's Church of the Vierzehnheiligen (begun 1743).

Rogers, Richard [b1933]: British Post-Modernist architect whose innovatory output includes the Paris Pompidou Centre (1977) and London's high-tech Lloyd's Building (1986).

Roll door (2.17): a type of door.

Roll moulding (3.01): a type of moulding.

Roman architecture (see style timechart): the building of ancient Rome with the emphasis on monumental public works (baths, amphitheatres and aqueducts, etc), military engineering (Hadrian's Wall) and rural villas. The Romans rediscovered brick and concrete to develop the first large vaults (groin variety invented) and domes by the 1st century BC. Relied on them and arches, more so than on columns, unlike the Greeks.

Romanesque (see style timechart): European-wide architectural style that broadly embraced building from the age of Charlemagne (c800) to the beginning of the Gothic. Characterised by rounded arches, clearly articulated ground plans and elevations, basilican-plan churches, and both barrel vaults and early rib vaults (Durham Cathedral, NE England).

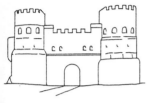

Roman architecture: Porta Ostiense (Gate of San Paolo), Aurelian Walls of Rome c280 (towers c310)

Rood (1.10): a cross or crucifix at the east end of a church's nave.

Rood loft (1.10): an area above a rood screen.

Rood screen (1.10): the screen at the east end of a nave which supports the rood (crucifix), and sometimes a rood loft.

Roof (1.13, 2.05): the protective cover on top of a building.

Roof light (2.14): a type of window.

Rope and feather (3.04): an ornamental motif.

Rope (cable) (3.04): an ornamental motif.

Rope torus (3.02): a type of moulding.

Rose banding (3.04): an ornamental motif.

Rose-en-soleil (3.06): an ornamental device.

Rose window (1.11): a type of circular window.

Rosette: a patera shaped like a rose.

Rotunda (2.05): a circular room or building.

Roughcast: a mixture of shingle and cement used as a coarse surfacing for building exteriors. Called Harling in Scotland.

Round billet (3.03): an ornamental motif.

Round horseshoe arch (2.13): a type of arch.

Roundel (3.09): a heraldic charge.

Roundel barry wavy (3.09): a heraldic charge.

Round moulding: (3.01) a type of moulding.

Round trefoil arch (2.13): a type of circular arch.

Round trifoliated arch (2.13): a type of circular arch.

RSJ: a rolled steel joist, used as a very versatile supporting member.

Rubble masonry/Rubblework (2.01): a type of dry stone walling.

Run (2.01): the tread of a staircase.

Rundbogenstil: German 19th century neo-Romanesque style.

Running dog: see Vitruvian scroll.

Ruskin, John [1819–1900]: Immensely influential British critic and architectural impressario whose writings such as *Seven Lamps of Architecture* (1849) takes to its extreme the 19th century worship of the purity and integrity of Gothic architecture and design.

Rusticated column (1.06): a type of column.

Rusticated stone dressing (2.01): a type of stone dressing.

Rustication (2.01): masonry cut in huge blocks with the surface left rough and unfinished (as opposed to ashlar).

Rustre (3.09): a heraldic charge.

Saarinen, Eero [1910–61]: Finnish-American modern architect whose works ranged from the severely International Modern style to a far more expressionistic modernism such as the TWA terminal at Kennedy Airport, New York (1956–62).

Sable (3.07): heraldic term for the colour blue.

Sacristy (1.09): a room in a church for keeping the priests' vestments

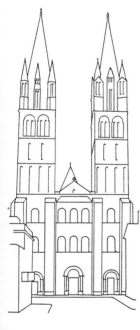

Romanesque: Abbaye-aux-Hommes (St Etienne), Caen, Normandy 1086

and the sacred vessels, and to serve as the former's robing room.

Saddleback roof (2.05): a pitched roof.

Saddle bars (2.14): small iron bars dividing glass panels in casement glazing.

Saint Andrew's cross bond: see English cross bond (2.03).

Saint Andrew's cross (3.06): an ornamental device.

Sally port: see Postern gate (1.07).

Sanctuary: (a) see presbytery (1.09). (b) generally the most sacred part of of a church or temple (1.01). (c) the right of a fugitive from justice to seek the protection, or sanctuary of the church. Abolished in England in the 17th century.

Sanctuary knocker (1.10): a fitment or ring on the door of a church that could be struck by a fugitive from the law.

Sanctus bell (1.08): a bell rung at the Sanctus, sometimes in a bell cote above the chancel arch, but usually a hand bell.

Sanguine (3.07): heraldic term for a blood-red colour.

Sarcophagus: see Tomb.

Sash frame (2.14): see Sash window.

Sash window (2.15): a type of window imported to England from Holland in the late 17th century, in which the frames slide up and down vertically supported on sash cords and a pulley.

Sawtooth roof (2.05): a type of roof.

Sawtooth wall (2.04): a pattern used on wooden walling.

Scaena/Scena (1.02): the back scene in a classical theatre.

Scagliola: imitation marker common in classical architecture in antiquity and the 17th/18th centuries.

Scalloped capital (1.06): a type of capital.

Scarp (1.07): in a fortress, the outer, often sloping sheer walls below the ramparts.

Scene building (1.02): see Scaena.

Scenographic perspective (3.10): a type of drawing projection.

Schinkel, Karl Friedrich [1781–1841]: versatile Prussian 19th century architect who studied under Gilly in Berlin. Much of his work was in pure Grecian neoclassical style, culminating in Berlin's Old Museum (1823–30), but he also worked in the Gothic and Romanesque (*Rundbogenstil*) styles and was interested in industrial developments.

Scissor brace (2.09): a traditional truss used as a roof support.

Scissors truss (2.09): modern version of a scissor brace.

Scotch bond (2.02): see American bond.

Scotia: (a) moulding on a classical pedestal (1.05). (b) a type of concave moulding (3.01).

Screen (1.10): (a) see rood screen (1.10). (b) in medieval domestic architecture a wooden screen at the end of a hall, usually supporting a gallery (1.13).

Screen door (2.17): a type of door with a fine mesh screen against insects.

Screwback (2.12): part of a segmental arch.

Scroll banding (3.04): an ornamental motif.

Scroll moulding (3.02): a type of moulding.

Sedilia (1.10): seats for the clergy on the south side of the choir aisle recessed into the church's masonry.

Segmental arch (2.13): an arch of which the shape represents only a fraction of a circle.

Seiren (3.05): an ornamental device.

Semi circular arch (2.13): a type of arch.

Semi circular stilted arch (2.13): a type of arch.

Serlian window 1537

Shingle style: Stoughton House, Cambridge Massachusetts 1882 by Henry H Richardson

Semy de lys (3.08): a division of a heraldic field.

Serlian/Serlain motif/Venetian window: a three-arched window common in 18th century English neoclassical architecture and taken from the writings of Sebastiano Serlio.

Serlio, Sebastiano [1475–1554]: Italian painter, architect and theorist whose book *L'Architettura* (1537–51) codified the classical orders. It became a prime source of both classical motif and Renaissance Italian styles for British and French architects.

Serpent nowed (3.05): an ornamental device.

Serpent vorant (3.05): an ornamental device.

Set off buttress (1.12): a type of buttress.

Severy (2.07): a vault division.

Sexpartite vault (2.07): a type of vault made up of six compartments.

Sgraffito: wall decoration consisting of a pattern scratched on a coat of white plaster which covers a layer of plaster in a different colour, thus giving a design in two colours.

Shaft: (a) the main body of a column (1.03, 1.06). (b) a small column attached to a pillar or pier (1.06).

Shaft ring: a stone ring binding a shaft [definition (b)] to a pillar or pier.

Shaft window (1.11): a type of window.

Shaped gable (2.08): a type of gable.

Sheathing wall (2.04): wooden walling.

Sheeting roof (2.08): asphalt roofing.

Shell: a self-supporting concrete shell or membrane constructed on the principle of an egg shell.

Shingle style: late 19th century American style of domestic architecture exemplified by Henry H Richardson's Stoughton House at Cambridge, Massachusetts (1882), with its open interior.

Shingle wall (2.04): a type of exterior wooden walling.

Shiplap wood siding (2.04): a type of wood siding.

Shoulder (2.12): part of an arch.

Shouldered arch (2.13): a type of circular arch.

Shutters/Jalousie (2.14): window blinds usually constructed from angled wood slats.

Shutting stile (2.16): a part of a door.

Side of a brick (2.02): a part of a brick.

Sill/Cell: (a) a projecting member under a window or door (1.12). (b) the horizontal base of a timber-framed wall (2.09).

Silver fir: common European wood for floorboards and joinery.

Simple drop wood siding (2.04): a type of wooden siding.

Single Flemish bond: a variation of Flemish bond (2.03).

Sinister (3.07): part of a heraldic shield.

Sinister base (3.07): part of a heraldic shield.

Sinister chief (3.07): part of a heraldic shield.

Sinister fess (3.07): part of a heraldic field.

Skeleton construction: construction based on a steel frame or a reinforced-concrete frame.

Skewback: see Screwback (2.12).

Skirt roof (2.05): a type of roof.

Skirting (2.10): (a) a wooden board around the floor edge a room to protect the bottom of the walls. (b) the lowest level of a wood-pannelled wall (2.09).

Skylight (2.05): a window in a roof to give light to a loft or room without other lighting.

Skyscraper: a very tall building of steel skeletal construction, developed in the USA from the 1880s.

Slate (2.08): a smooth-grained rock split into layers and used for roofing.

Sliding door (2.17): a door that slides open horizontally.

Sliding window (2.15): a window that slides open horizontally.

Slype (1.09): a passageway in a church from the cloisters to the transept and chapter house.

Soane, Sir John [1753–1837]: ingenious and original English neoclassical architect whose Bank of England (1792–1827: now mainly gone) used a supremely simple version of classicism. His idiosyncrasy and range of taste is best seen at his own home, now the Sir John Soane Museum in Lincoln's Inn Fields, London (1812–13).

Soffit: see Intrados.

Solar (1.13): an upper room in a medieval house.

Soldier (2.02): a position in brickwork.

Sole plate (2.10): a part of a wood-framed structure.

Solea (1.09): a platform connecting a bema and an ambo in a Byzantine church. See Ambo and Bema.

Solomonic column (1.06): a twisted column.

Sopraporta: a painting above a doorway, designed as a decorative whole.

Space-frame: large-scale framework systems, used in modern architecture to cover large spaces, such as Buckminster Fuller's domes.

Span: the width of an arch.

Spandrel (1.12): the triangular space formed by the rising of an arch and the rectangle of the bay or doorway into which it fits.

Spanish tile (2.08): a type of roofing tile.

Spiral fluted column (1.06): a type of column.

Spiral staircase (2.11): a type of staircase.

Spire (1.08): a steep pointed structure soaring from a tower or roof of a religious or public building.

Spired turret (2.05): a turret with a spire.

Split brick (2.02): a type of brick.

Spout (1.08): a carved stone spout for throwing the water off the roofs of medieval buildings.

Spring line (2.12): the point at which an arch unites with its support.

Sprocket (2.09): a timber running off a roof's rafters to act as an eave.

Spruce: light, versatile, North American softwood.

Spur (1.06): a small piece of ornamental foliage on the corners of a rectangular plinth surmounted by a column.

Square billet banding (3.03): an ornamental motif.

Squinch arch (2.05, 2.06): arch used in the support of a dome.

Squint (1.10): a slit in a medieval wall or pier to allow sight of the altar from areas hidden by masonry.

Stadium: a sports ground for athletics.

Stafford knot (3.06): an ornamental device.

Stag at gaze (3.05): an ornamental device.

Stag at speed (3.05): an ornamental device.

Staggered wood (2.04): a pattern in wooden walling.

Stag's head cabossed (3.05): an ornamental device.

Stag trippant (3.05): an ornamental device.

Stained glass (1.11): bible narrative, the life of Christ and the saints, memorial plaques and moral homilies depicted in multi-coloured glass between the tracery of windows in medieval and more recent churches. The earliest surviving examples are five windows in Augsburg Cathedral, South Germany, dated c1125.

Staircase (1.13, 1.15, 2.11): a flight of steps.

Stadium: Stadium of Domitian, Rome AD86

©DIAGRAM

Stave church: Heddal,
Norway 1250

Stoa: Assos, Asia Minor,
Hellenistic

Strainer arch: Wells
Cathedral, Somerset, 1338

Swag: on a carpet

Stairwell (2.11): a shaft in a building that contains a dogleg or a double return staircase.

Stanchion: a vertical supporting member of a building.

Star (3.06): heraldic device.

Stave church (see style timechart): Scandinavian timber-framed and timber-walled churches built from the 11th century onwards.

Steeple (1.08): the tower of a church with its spire, lantern or other superstructure.

Stepped flashing (2.07): a roof finish along the edges to prevent rain seeping through.

Stiff-leaf capital (1.06): a type of column capital.

Stilted arch (2.12): a type of circular arch.

Stirling, James [b1926]: internationally renowned Post-Modern British architect whose uncompromising use of form and material has brought him close to Brutalism; as at the History Faculty Building, Cambridge (1965–8). His *Staatsgallerie*, Stuttgart, W Germany is nonetheless a popular success.

Stoa: in Greek architecture a covered colonnade or hall (often with shops) open on the colonnaded side and sometimes two-storied.

Stock brick: the basic brick made in any given region, ie London stock brick.

Stop champfer/Broach stop (1.12): the point at which a champfer ends and the vertical support's shapes reverts to the rectangular.

Stops: carved projecting stones at the end of mouldings and string courses.

Storage cupboard (1.15): a cupboard.

Store cellar (1.13): a cellar.

Storey/Story: the main levels or floors of a building numbered from ground-level up.

Stoup (1.10): see Holy water stone.

Straight flight staircase: the simplest type of staircase.

Strainer arch: remedial arches inserted across a nave or aisle to prevent subsidence. The best known examples are at the crossing of Wells Cathedral, England.

Strapwork: an ornamental motif.

Stretcher (2.02): a position in brickwork.

String course (1.12): a moulded projecting horizontal band on the exterior of a wall.

Strings/Wall stringer (2.11): the sloping sides of a staircase that carry the treads (steps).

Strut (2.09): part of a roof support.

Stucco: smooth plasterwork used on ceilings and on the outside of buildings as a facing material.

Stud (2.10): a part of a wood-framed structure.

Study: a room for intellectual work.

Stylobate (1.03): the upper step of a platform supporting a colonnade in Greek architecture.

Sullivan, Louis Henry [1856–1924]: American Chicago-based architect and decorator who, with Dankmar Adler, designed over 100 buildings (1880–95) including revolutionary early steel-framed skyscrapers.

Superimposed orders: the mixture of Doric, Ionic and Corinthian orders in one building.

Sussex garden wall bond: see Flemish garden wall (2.03).

Swag: a decorative motif.

Swing door (2.17): a door that opens by swinging.

Synagogue: a Jewish place of worship.

Tabernacle: Renaissance by Florentine sculptor Desiderio da Settignano

Temple: Ionic Temple of Artemis, Ephesus, Asia Minor c300BC by Dinocrates of Alexandria

Terrace: (b): Hanover Terrace, Regent's Park, London 1828 by Nash

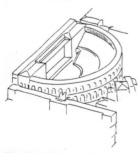

Theatre: Theatre of Balbus, Rome 13BC

Tholos: Athens Agora before 450BC

Systyle (1.05): a system of columniation in which the intervals between columns are twice the diameter of the column.

Tabernacle: (a) the portable sanctuary in which the ancient Israelites carried the Ark of the Covenant. (b) an ornamental cupboard in a medieval or Catholic church containing the Eucharist (1.10). (c) a niche, recess or covered altar acting as a shrine.

Tablet flower banding (3.03): an ornamental motif.

Tablinum (1.01): in Roman domestic architecture, a reception room opening on the atrium.

Talus (1.07): in military architecture, a rampart's rearward slope or any earthwork slope.

Tange, Kenzo [b1913]: leading Japanese modern architect, engineer, town planner, especially for his work in Japan's major cities since 1950 and designing Nigeria's crescent-shaped capital-to-be Abuja.

Tatlin, Vladimir [1885–1953]: Russian abstract painter, sculptor, theatre/industrial designer and visionary architect whose grandiose project for a Monument to the Third International (1919) was the key architectural concept of Constructivism.

Tau cross (3.06, 3.09): a heraldic charge.

Teak: a very resistant oriental hardwood.

Telamon (1.06): see Atlanta.

Telford, Thomas [1757–1834]: prolific Scottish engineer, architect and pioneer in the use of cast iron. He built churches, canals, docks, aqueducts, roads, and perhaps most notably, bridges such as the Menai Straits Suspension Bridge (1819–26).

Template/Templet: a metal or wooden frame for testing the shape of building materials.

Temple (1.01): a place of worship particularly associated with classical Greek architecture.

Tenia (1.03): a moulding at the top of an architrave.

Tenne (3.07): heraldic term for the colour orange.

Tenon: see Mortice and Tenon.

Tepidarium (1.02): the warm room in a Roman baths.

Term: an ornamental pedestal surmounted by figure.

Terrace: (a) a level area and walkway in front of a house. (b) a line of houses built as a single unit of design.

Terazzo: see Terrace (a).

Terreplein: in military architecture, the broad platform of a rampart or a covered way.

Terry, Quinlan [b1937]: modern British neoclassical architect noteworthy for country house work and the Richmond Thameside complex (1984).

Tester: a canopy.

Tetrastyle (1.03): a portico with four columns.

Thatch (2.07): a straw roof.

Theatre (1.02): a building designed for the performance of plays.

Thermae (1.02): Roman public baths.

Thermal window: (a) a semi-circular high-level window found in Roman bath buildings. (b) an insulated window.

Tholos: a circular domed building.

Three-centred arch (2.13): a type of circular arch.

Three quarters (2.02): a shape of brick.

Threshold (2.16): part of a doorway.

Thrust: the transference of weight from an arch or vault to the side walls and buttresses.

Thumb: see Moulding.

Thumb, Michael [d1690]: German architect and founder of the

©DIAGRAM

Tomb: Hellenistic at Dougga (Thugga), Tunisia

Triumphal arch: Arch of Titus, Rome AD82

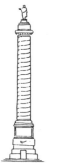

Triumphal column: Column of Marcus Aurelius, Rome cAD180

Trophy: Trajan's Trophy, Adamclisi, Romania AD109

Tudor: Clock Court Entrance, Hampton Court Palace c1520

Voralberger school, and a dynasty, of architects who created and perfected Baroque and Rococo building in South Germany.

Tie beam (2.09): the key lowest member of a truss used in roof support.

Tiercerons (2.07): a division line in vaulting.

Tile: a thin rectangular slab used in roofing, flooring or walling.

Tilehanging: overlapping layers of roof tiles.

Timber: wood.

Timber framing/Timber built/Half Timber (2.09): the use of timber for creating the structure of a wall.

Toilet: a lavatory.

Tomb: a place for the burial of a corpse.

Tongue and groove (2.04): a wood siding.

Top cripple (2.10): a part of a wood-framed structure.

Top panel (2.16): part of a door.

Top rail (2.16): part of a door.

Torus (1.05, 3.01): a convex moulding at the base of a column.

Tower (1.07, 1.08): a very tall structure, usually square or circular, designed for observation, communication and defence.

Town planning: the art of laying out a city or urban area according to design and sociological considerations.

Trabeated: building designed on vertical/horizontal (post and lintel) basis, rather than arcuated (with arches, vaults and domes).

Tracery (1.11): the masonry designs within a medieval window.

Trachelion (1.05): the neck of a Doric column.

Transept (1.09): the area of a cross-shaped church intersecting with the nave of the crossing.

Transitional Style: architectural style halfway between Romanesque and Gothic.

Transom (1.11): horizontal masonry division of a window.

Transverse ridge (2.07): division of a vault.

Transverse ridge rib (2.07): division of a vault.

Traverse: in military architecture, a trench or covered way bay partition to protect troops from flanking fire.

Trefoil: see Foil.

Trefoil slipped (3.06): an ornamental device.

Triangular arch (2.13): a type of pointed arch.

Triangulation: any construction based on a continuous series of triangles to give stability.

Tribune: (a) a raised platform. (b) a basilican apse. (c) a church gallery.

Triclinium (1.01): dining room in a Roman house.

Triforium (1.10): an arcaded passage above the nave of a medieval church.

Triglyph (1.03, 1.05): part of a Doric frieze.

Trimetric projection (3.10): a drawing projection.

Triquetre (3.05): an ornamental device.

Tristyle (1.03): a portico with three columns.

Triumphal arch: a Roman monumental gateway, much imitated in the Renaissance and since, to celebrate military victory or prowess, eg Arc de Triomphe (1806–35).

Triumphal column: a decorated column to celebrate a military victory, eg Trajan's Column, Rome (AD113).

Trophy: an ornamented display of captured arms and armour.

Trumeau: a vertical stone central support for the pediment of a doorway.

Truss (2.09): an arrangement of timbers supporting a roof.

Tudor (see style timechart): English architecture during the reigns of the five Tudor monarchs, which saw both the final flowering of English

Perpendicular Style, and the introduction of Romanesque motifs to British architecture; eg King Henry VII's Chapel, Westminster Abbey (1502 onwards) and Burghley House (1577–87, Renaissance detailing).

Tudor arch (2.13): a type of four-centred pointed arch common in Tudor England.

Tudor flower: an ornamental device.

Turnstile door (2.17): a type of revolving door.

Trochylua: see Scotia.

Tufa: a volcanic stone much used by the Romans.

Turrer/Touret/Turette (2.05): a very small tower.

Tuscan order (1.04): a derivation of the Doric order.

Two dolphins (3.05): an ornamental device.

Two-headed eagle (3.05): an ornamental device.

Tympanum: (a) the triangular space within a pediment (1.03). (b) the semi-circular space above the lintel in arched doorway.

Upper cruck (2.09): a type of roof support.

Urdy (3.08): a division line in heraldry.

Vair (3.07): a heraldic tincture.

Valley (2.05): a type of roof.

Valley flashing (2.08): a roof finish in its groove to prevent water leaking through.

Vanbrugh, Sir John [1664–1726]: English officer, playwright and leading Baroque architect. Without any formal training he became Wren's chief assistant and then the builder, with Hawksmoor, of such grandiose country houses as Castle Howard (1699–1726) and Blenheim Palace (1705–22), edifices on a truly continental scale unrivalled elsewhere in England.

Vane: see Weathervane.

Vauban, Sébastien Le Prestre de [1633–1707]: French fortress builder, siege engineer and marshal of France who is the greatest name in military architecture. Refortified or built from scratch 160 fortresses, directed over 50 successful sieges for Louis XIV. Devised the casemated bastion tower in 1687 and a powder magazine (standard till 1874). Founded France's engineering corps (1690), the modern world's first such permanent professional body.

Vault (2.07): an arched ceiling or roof.

Vaultstone (2.12): part below the capstone of an arch.

Vaulting shaft (2.07): a part of a vault.

Velde, Henri Van de [1863–1957]: Belgian painter and Art Nouveau architect. In 1895 he designed for Bing's shop L'Art Nouveau in Paris, and settled at Berlin where his new style was instantly popular. Rebuilt the Art School (1904) and the School of Arts and Crafts (1907) in Weimar which developed into the Bauhaus.

Venetian arch (2.13): a type of circular arch.

Veranda: an open-roofed balcony.

Verge (2.05): part of a roof.

Vermiculated (2.01): a type of stone dressing.

Vert (3.07): heraldic term for the colour green.

Vestibule (1.01, 1.02): an entrance room or ante-chamber.

Vestry: see Sacristy.

Viaduct: a series of arches which carry a road, canal or railway over a valley or low ground.

Vignette (3.04): an ornamental motif.

Villa: (a) a Roman or Renaissance country house. (b) a modern detached house.

Vitruvian opening: a design of doorway or window.

Viaduct: Long Key, Florida, 1890s

©DIAGRAM

Vitruvian scroll (3.04): a classical ornamental motif.

Vitruvius Pollio, Marcus (active 46–c13BC): an indifferent Roman architect whose treatise in ten books, *De architectura*, the only such work to survive from antiquity, was rediscovered in the Renaissance and became an endless and fertile source of inspiration for classical architects and designers.

Voided cross (3.09): a heraldic charge.

Volute: (a) the scroll on an Ionic column (1.05). (b) the same in motif (3.04).

Vomitoria: an annexe to a Roman dining room for relieving oneself of surplus food.

Vise (2.11): see Wreath.

Voussoir (2.12): part of an arch.

Wagon vault: see Vault.

Wainscot (2.10): wooden panelling as a wall surface.

Waist (2.11): part of a staircase.

Wake knot (3.06): an ornamental device.

Wall plate (2.08): part of a roof.

Wall stringer (2.11): see Strings.

Ward: see Bailey.

Watchtower (1.07): a tall tower for military observation, often part of a castle.

Waterleaf: see Capital.

Waterleaf and tongue/scroll (3.04): a type of motif.

Wattle and daub (2.10): wall construction, sometimes used with timber framing, consisting of thin strips of wood (laths) bound with clay or mud.

Wave (3.03): a type of motif.

Wavy/Undy (3.08): a division line in heraldry.

Weatherboard (2.13, 2.15): (a) the lower part of a window to keep out rain (2.13). (b) the lower part of a door to keep out rain (2.16).

Weatherboarding (2.04): an exterior wall surface of overlapping horizontal board, used on timber-framed houses.

Weathercock: see Vane.

Weathervane (1.08): see Vane.

Web (2.07): the bay of a vault.

Webb, Philip Speakman [1831–1915]: English domestic architect and designer, friend of William Morris and leading figure of the Arts and Crafts Movement. For Morris he built the Red House, Bexley, Kent (1859), the start of a vogue for rustic country houses until the 1890s in which Webb and Richard Norman Shaw (1831–1912) were foremost.

Westwork: the western end of a Carolingian or Romanesque church.

Wheel window: see Rose window.

Wicket: a small gate or door.

Window (1.11, 2.14, 2.15): a wall opening to let in light.

Window frame (2.10): a window surround.

Window sill (2.10): part of a window.

Wooden balustrade (2.16): a wooden railing.

Wood girder (2.10): a part of a wood-framed structure.

Wood sheathing (2.10): a part of a wood-framed structure.

Wreath staircase (2.11): see Vise.

Wren, Sir Christopher [1632–1723]: Pre-eminent English architect, also a scientist of distinction in London and Oxford, and an MP. In 1665–6 he was in Paris and met Bernini, Mansart and Le Vau. In 1667 he became a surveyor under the Rebuilding Act after the Great Fire of London (1666) and in 1669 was made Surveyor-General of the King's Works. His

Westwork: Abbey Church, Corvey on the Weser, Germany 885

scholarly, refined, detailed and inventive Baroque style was intensely English as at St Paul's Cathedral, London, and in more than 30 other new City churches. His grandest secular building was the Greenwich Hospital (1696 onwards).

Wright, Frank Lloyd [1869–1959]: constantly inventive and most famous American modern architect. His career spans the Sullivan era in Chicago and the postwar power of imperial US architecture – from his many early Chicago private houses (eg Robie House 1905) to the office skyscrapers of Bartlesville, Oklahoma (1955). He was very influential in England and Europe at the turn of the century.

Wyvern (3.05): an ornamental device.

Xenodochium: a room in a monstery for entertaining strangers.

Xystus: see Ambulatory.

Y form roof (2.05): a type of roof.

Zig zag (3.03): an ornamental motif.

Z shape metal tie (2.02): a type of metal tie.

STYLE TIMECHART TO 1400

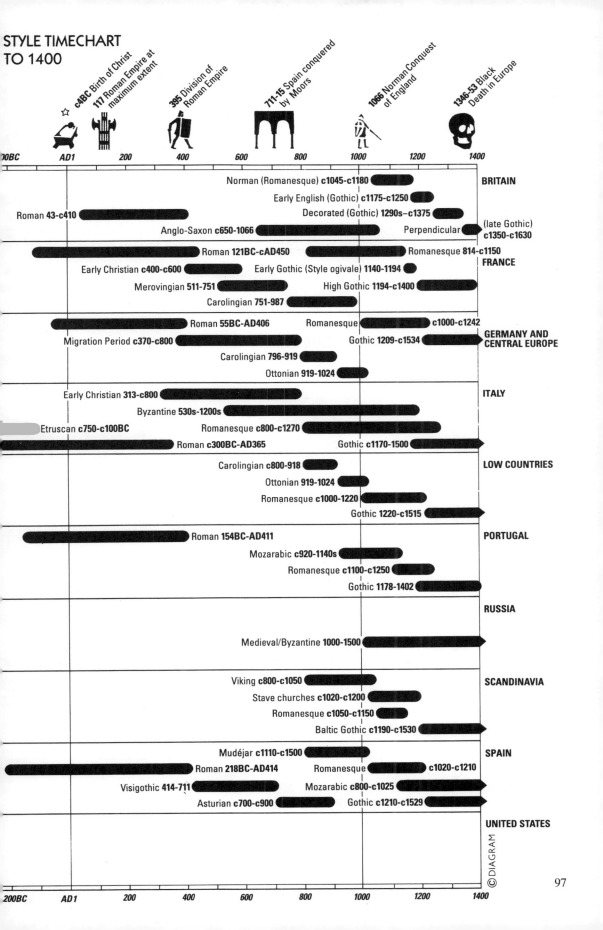

☆ **c4BC** Birth of Christ
117 Roman Empire at maximum extent
395 Division of Roman Empire
711-15 Spain conquered by Moors
1066 Norman Conquest of England
1346-53 Black Death in Europe

200BC — AD1 — 200 — 400 — 600 — 800 — 1000 — 1200 — 1400

BRITAIN

Norman (Romanesque) **c1045-c1180**
Early English (Gothic) **c1175-c1250**
Roman **43-c410**
Decorated (Gothic) **1290s-c1375**
Anglo-Saxon **c650-1066**
Perpendicular (late Gothic) **c1350-c1630**

FRANCE

Roman **121BC-cAD450**
Romanesque **814-c1150**
Early Christian **c400-c600**
Early Gothic (Style ogivale) **1140-1194**
Merovingian **511-751**
High Gothic **1194-c1400**
Carolingian **751-987**

GERMANY AND CENTRAL EUROPE

Roman **55BC-AD406**
Romanesque **c1000-c1242**
Migration Period **c370-c800**
Gothic **1209-c1534**
Carolingian **796-919**
Ottonian **919-1024**

ITALY

Early Christian **313-c800**
Byzantine **530s-1200s**
Etruscan **c750-c100BC**
Romanesque **c800-c1270**
Roman **c300BC-AD365**
Gothic **c1170-1500**

LOW COUNTRIES

Carolingian **c800-918**
Ottonian **919-1024**
Romanesque **c1000-1220**
Gothic **1220-c1515**

PORTUGAL

Roman **154BC-AD411**
Mozarabic **c920-1140s**
Romanesque **c1100-c1250**
Gothic **1178-1402**

RUSSIA

Medieval/Byzantine **1000-1500**

SCANDINAVIA

Viking **c800-c1050**
Stave churches **c1020-c1200**
Romanesque **c1050-c1150**
Baltic Gothic **c1190-c1530**

SPAIN

Mudéjar **c1110-c1500**
Roman **218BC-AD414**
Romanesque **c1020-c1210**
Visigothic **414-711**
Mozarabic **c800-c1025**
Asturian **c700-c900**
Gothic **c1210-c1529**

UNITED STATES

©DIAGRAM

STYLE TIMECHART
1400–1800

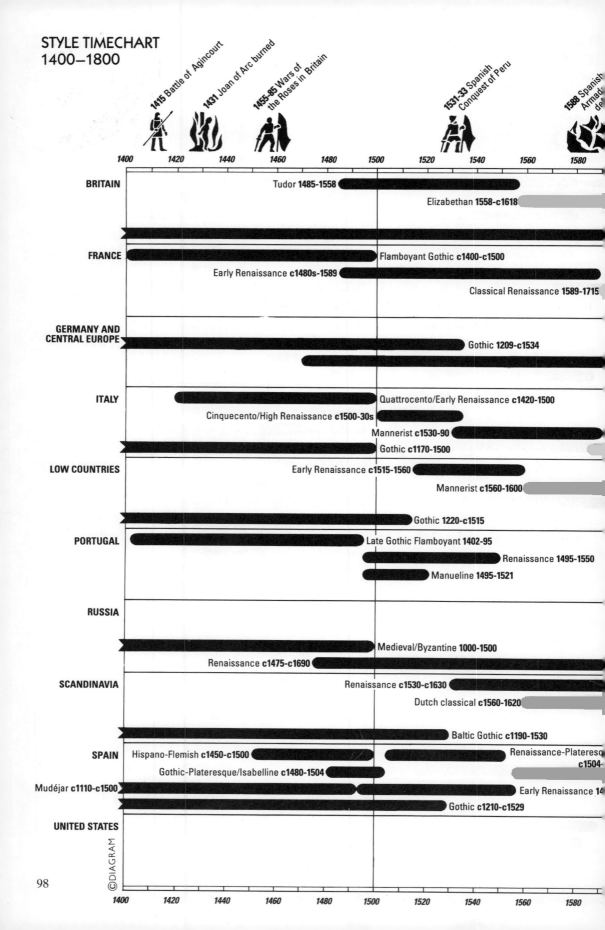

1415 Battle of Agincourt

1431 Joan of Arc burned

1455-85 Wars of the Roses in Britain

1531-33 Spanish Conquest of Peru

1588 Spanish Armada defeat

1400 1420 1440 1460 1480 1500 1520 1540 1560 1580

BRITAIN

Tudor **1485-1558**

Elizabethan **1558-c1618**

FRANCE

Flamboyant Gothic **c1400-c1500**

Early Renaissance **c1480s-1589**

Classical Renaissance **1589-1715**

GERMANY AND CENTRAL EUROPE

Gothic **1209-c1534**

ITALY

Quattrocento/Early Renaissance **c1420-1500**

Cinquecento/High Renaissance **c1500-30s**

Mannerist **c1530-90**

Gothic **c1170-1500**

LOW COUNTRIES

Early Renaissance **c1515-1560**

Mannerist **c1560-1600**

Gothic **1220-c1515**

PORTUGAL

Late Gothic Flamboyant **1402-95**

Renaissance **1495-1550**

Manueline **1495-1521**

RUSSIA

Medieval/Byzantine **1000-1500**

Renaissance **c1475-c1690**

SCANDINAVIA

Renaissance **c1530-c1630**

Dutch classical **c1560-1620**

Baltic Gothic **c1190-1530**

SPAIN

Hispano-Flemish **c1450-c1500**

Renaissance-Plateresco **c1504-**

Gothic-Plateresque/Isabelline **c1480-1504**

Mudéjar **c1110-c1500**

Early Renaissance **14**

Gothic **c1210-c1529**

UNITED STATES

©DIAGRAM

1400 1420 1440 1460 1480 1500 1520 1540 1560 1580

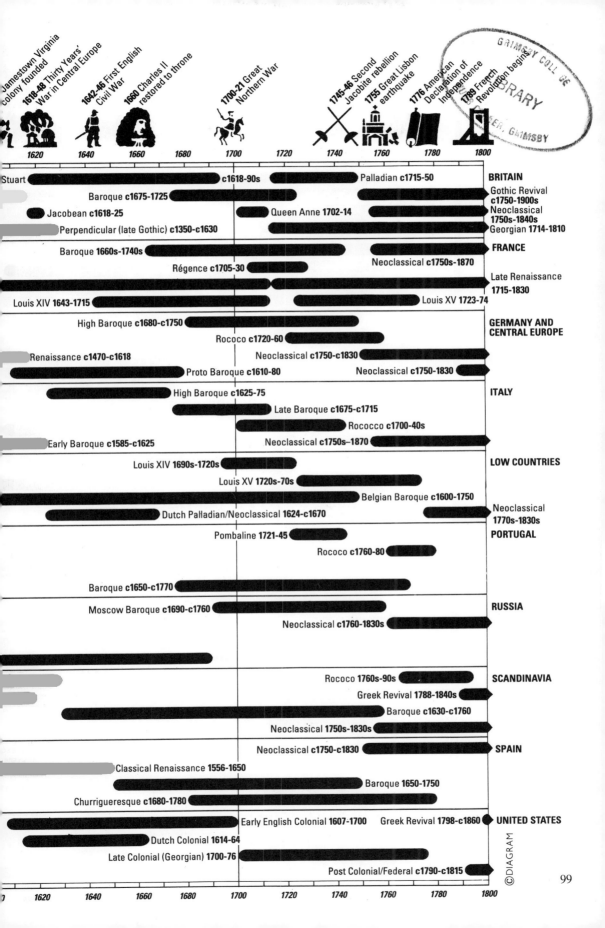

Jamestown Virginia colony founded
1618-48 Thirty Years' War in Central Europe
1642-46 First English Civil War
1660 Charles II restored to throne
1700-21 Great Northern War
1745-46 Second Jacobite rebellion
1755 Great Lisbon earthquake
1776 American Declaration of Independence
1789 French Revolution begins

1620 1640 1660 1680 1700 1720 1740 1760 1780 1800

BRITAIN
- Stuart c1618-90s
- Palladian c1715-50
- Baroque c1675-1725
- Gothic Revival c1750-1900s
- Jacobean c1618-25
- Queen Anne 1702-14
- Neoclassical 1750s-1840s
- Perpendicular (late Gothic) c1350-c1630
- Georgian 1714-1810

FRANCE
- Baroque 1660s-1740s
- Neoclassical c1750s-1870
- Régence c1705-30
- Late Renaissance 1715-1830
- Louis XIV 1643-1715
- Louis XV 1723-74

GERMANY AND CENTRAL EUROPE
- High Baroque c1680-c1750
- Rococo c1720-60
- Renaissance c1470-c1618
- Neoclassical c1750-c1830
- Proto Baroque c1610-80
- Neoclassical c1750-1830

ITALY
- High Baroque c1625-75
- Late Baroque c1675-c1715
- Rococco c1700-40s
- Early Baroque c1585-c1625
- Neoclassical c1750s–1870

LOW COUNTRIES
- Louis XIV 1690s-1720s
- Louis XV 1720s-70s
- Belgian Baroque c1600-1750
- Dutch Palladian/Neoclassical 1624-c1670
- Neoclassical 1770s-1830s

PORTUGAL
- Pombaline 1721-45
- Rococo c1760-80
- Baroque c1650-c1770

RUSSIA
- Moscow Baroque c1690-c1760
- Neoclassical c1760-1830s

SCANDINAVIA
- Rococo 1760s-90s
- Greek Revival 1788-1840s
- Baroque c1630-c1760
- Neoclassical 1750s-1830s

SPAIN
- Neoclassical c1750-c1830
- Classical Renaissance 1556-1650
- Baroque 1650-1750
- Churrigueresque c1680-1780

UNITED STATES
- Early English Colonial 1607-1700
- Greek Revival 1798-c1860
- Dutch Colonial 1614-64
- Late Colonial (Georgian) 1700-76
- Post Colonial/Federal c1790-c1815

©DIAGRAM

1620 1640 1660 1680 1700 1720 1740 1760 1780 1800

99

STYLE TIMECHART
1800–1990

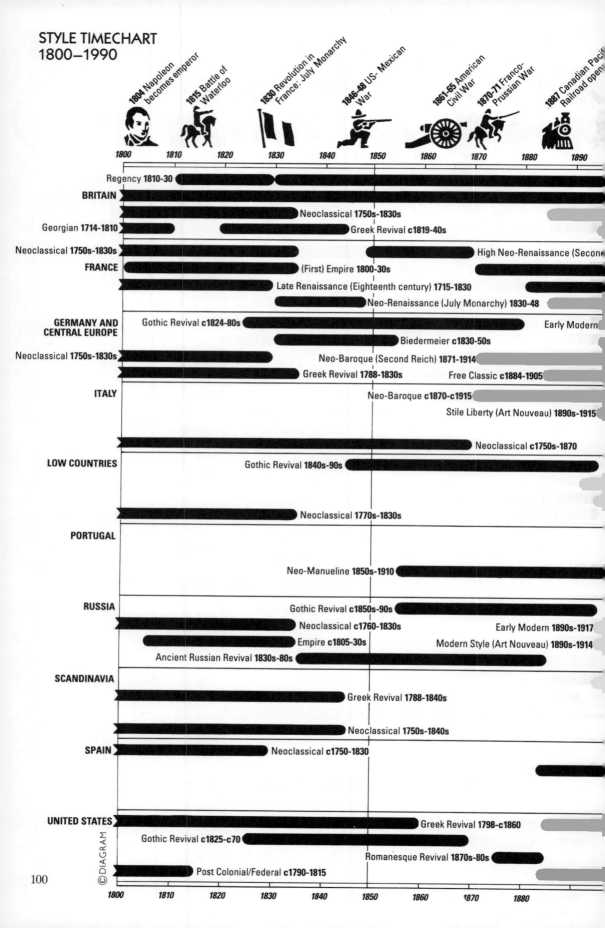

1804 Napoleon becomes emperor

1815 Battle of Waterloo

1830 Revolution in France: July Monarchy

1846-48 US- Mexican War

1861-65 American Civil War

1870-71 Franco-Prussian War

1887 Canadian Pacific Railroad open

1800 1810 1820 1830 1840 1850 1860 1870 1880 1890

BRITAIN

Regency **1810-30**

Georgian **1714-1810**

Neoclassical **1750s-1830s**

Greek Revival **c1819-40s**

FRANCE

Neoclassical **1750s-1830s**

High Neo-Renaissance (Secon

(First) Empire **1800-30s**

Late Renaissance (Eighteenth century) **1715-1830**

Neo-Renaissance (July Monarchy) **1830-48**

GERMANY AND CENTRAL EUROPE

Gothic Revival **c1824-80s**

Early Modern

Biedermeier **c1830-50s**

Neoclassical **1750s-1830s**

Neo-Baroque (Second Reich) **1871-1914**

Greek Revival **1788-1830s**

Free Classic **c1884-1905**

ITALY

Neo-Baroque **c1870-c1915**

Stile Liberty (Art Nouveau) **1890s-1915**

Neoclassical **c1750s-1870**

LOW COUNTRIES

Gothic Revival **1840s-90s**

Neoclassical **1770s-1830s**

PORTUGAL

Neo-Manueline **1850s-1910**

RUSSIA

Gothic Revival **c1850s-90s**

Neoclassical **c1760-1830s**

Early Modern **1890s-1917**

Empire **c1805-30s**

Modern Style (Art Nouveau) **1890s-1914**

Ancient Russian Revival **1830s-80s**

SCANDINAVIA

Greek Revival **1788-1840s**

Neoclassical **1750s-1840s**

SPAIN

Neoclassical **c1750-1830**

UNITED STATES

Greek Revival **1798-c1860**

Gothic Revival **c1825-c70**

Romanesque Revival **1870s-80s**

Post Colonial/Federal **c1790-1815**

© DIAGRAM

100

1800 1810 1820 1830 1840 1850 1860 1870 1880

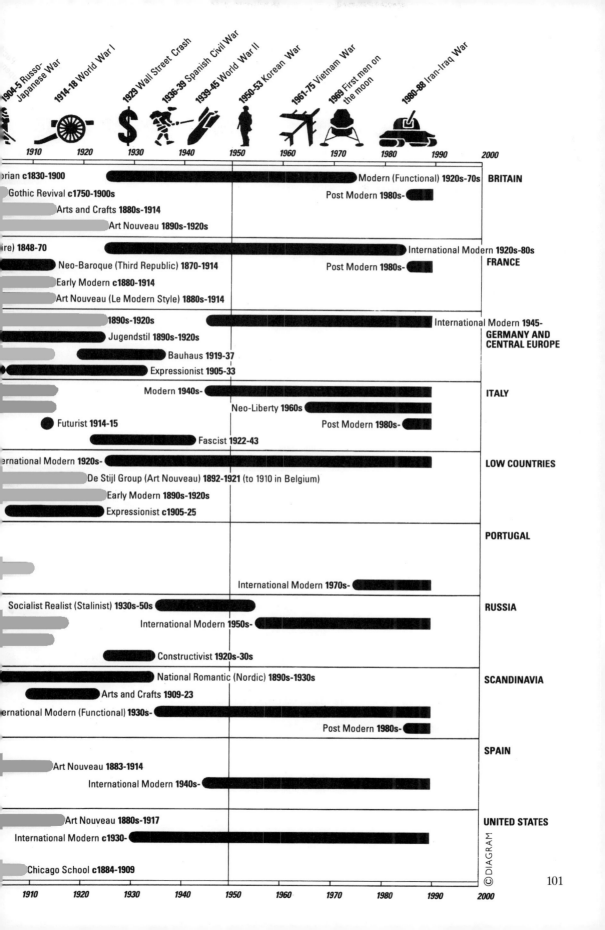

1904-5 Russo-Japanese War   **1914-18 World War I**   **1929 Wall Street Crash**   **1936-39 Spanish Civil War**   **1939-45 World War II**   **1950-53 Korean War**   **1961-75 Vietnam War**   **1969 First men on the moon**   **1980-88 Iran-Iraq War**

1910   1920   1930   1940   1950   1960   1970   1980   1990   2000

...orian **c1830-1900** — Modern (Functional) **1920s-70s**   **BRITAIN**
Gothic Revival **c1750-1900s** — Post Modern **1980s-**
Arts and Crafts **1880s-1914**
Art Nouveau **1890s-1920s**

...ire) **1848-70** — International Modern **1920s-80s**
Neo-Baroque (Third Republic) **1870-1914** — Post Modern **1980s-**   **FRANCE**
Early Modern **c1880-1914**
Art Nouveau (Le Modern Style) **1880s-1914**

1890s-1920s — International Modern **1945-**
Jugendstil **1890s-1920s**   **GERMANY AND CENTRAL EUROPE**
Bauhaus **1919-37**
Expressionist **1905-33**

Modern **1940s-**   **ITALY**
Neo-Liberty **1960s**
Futurist **1914-15**   Post Modern **1980s-**
Fascist **1922-43**

...ernational Modern **1920s-**   **LOW COUNTRIES**
De Stijl Group (Art Nouveau) **1892-1921** (to 1910 in Belgium)
Early Modern **1890s-1920s**
Expressionist **c1905-25**

PORTUGAL
International Modern **1970s-**

Socialist Realist (Stalinist) **1930s-50s**   **RUSSIA**
International Modern **1950s-**

Constructivist **1920s-30s**
National Romantic (Nordic) **1890s-1930s**   **SCANDINAVIA**
Arts and Crafts **1909-23**
...ernational Modern (Functional) **1930s-**
Post Modern **1980s-**

SPAIN
Art Nouveau **1883-1914**
International Modern **1940s-**

Art Nouveau **1880s-1917**   **UNITED STATES**
International Modern **c1930-**
Chicago School **c1884-1909**

1910   1920   1930   1940   1950   1960   1970   1980   1990   2000

ARCHITECTS' LIFELINES 2630BC – AD1700

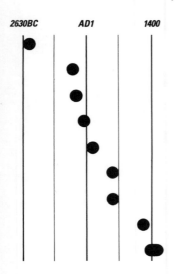

2630BC   AD1   1400

2630BC–AD1400

1 **Imhotep** active c2630–2611BC
   Egypt; Old Kingdom pyramidal

2 **Callicrates** active 449–425BC
   Athens; Doric and Ionic

3 **Ictinus** active c447–430BC
   Greece; Doric and Ionic

4 **Marcus Vitruvius Pollio** active 46–c13BC
   Italy; Classical

5 **Apollodorus of Damascus** active c98–c130
   Roman Empire; Classical

6 **Anthemius of Tralles** active 532–7
   Constantinople; Byzantine

7 **Isidore of Miletus** active 532–7
   Constantinople; Byzantine

8 **Arnolfo di Cambio** c1245–1302
   Florence 1266–1302; Gothic

9 **Filippo Brunelleschi** 1377–1446
   Florence Cathedral 1404–46; Early Renaissance

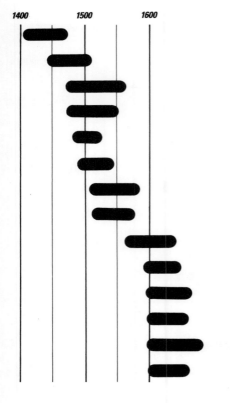

1400   1500   1600

1400–1600

1 **Leon Battista Alberti** 1404–72
   Rome, Rimini, Florence, Mantua 1446–72; Early Renaissance

2 **Donato Bramante** 1444–1514
   Milan, Pavia, Rome c1479–1514; High Renaissance

3 **Michelangelo Buonarotti** 1475–1564
   Rome, Florence 1514–64; High Renaissance/Mannerist

4 **Sebastiano Serlio** 1475–1554
   Rome, Venice, France 1514–51; High Renaissance

5 **Raphael (Raffaello Sanzio)** 1483–1520
   Rome 1509–20; High Renaissance

6 **Giulio Romano** 1492/9–1546
   Rome, Mantua 1521–46; High Renaissance

7 **Andrea Palladio** 1508–80
   Vicenza and Veneto 1540–80; Palladian

8 **Philibert Delorme** 1510/15–70
   France 1536–70; Early Renaissance

9 **Inigo Jones** 1573–1652
   England, Wales 1608–c49; Stuart Renaissance

10 **Jacob van Campen** 1595–1657
   Amsterdam, Haarlem 1637–57; Palladian

11 **Pietro Berrettini da Cortona** 1596–1669
   Rome 1626–69; High Baroque

12 **François Mansart** 1598–1666
   France 1623–55; Classical Renaissance

13 **Gianlorenzo Bernini** 1598–1680
   Rome 1624–c74; High Baroque

14 **Francesco Borromini** 1599–1667
   Rome 1633–67; High Baroque

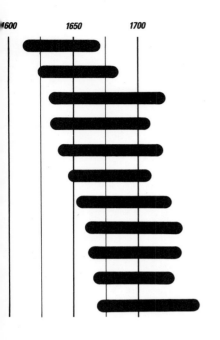

1600–1670

1 **Louis Le Vau** 1612–70
   Paris, Vaux-le-Vicomte, Versailles c1640–70; Classical Renaissance/Baroque

2 **Guarino Guarini** 1624–83
   Italy, Paris, Lisbon, Prague, Vienna 1641–83; Baroque

3 **Sir Christopher Wren** 1632–1723
   Oxford, Cambridge, London 1662–1714; Baroque

4 **Sébastien le Prestre Vauban** 1633–1707
   France, Low Countries, Piedmont, Germany 1664–1701; Baroque Military

5 **Carlo Fontana** 1638–1714
   Rome, Genoa, Ravenna, Loyola (Spain) 1662–1708; Baroque

6 **Jules Hardouin-Mansart** 1646–1708
   France 1674–1708; Baroque

7 **Johann Bernhard Fischer von Ehrlach** 1656–1723
   Austria, Czechoslovakia, Poland 1687–1723; Baroque

8 **Nicholas Hawksmoor** 1661–1736
   England c1679–1736; Baroque

9 **Matthaeus Daniel Pöppelmann** 1662–1736
   Saxony c1685–1736; Baroque

10 **Sir John Vanbrugh** 1664–1726
   England 1699–1726; Baroque

11 **Johann Lucas von Hildebrandt** 1668–1745
   Austria, Bohemia, Hungary, Germany 1697–1737; Baroque

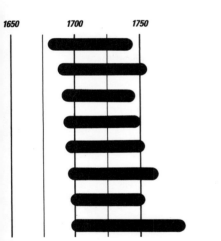

1670–1700

1 **Thomas Archer** 1678–1743
   England 1703–30; Baroque/Palladian

2 **James Gibbs** 1682–1754
   England, Ireland 1711–49; Mannerist/Baroque

3 **William Kent** 1685–1748
   England c1724–48; Palladian

4 **Cosmas Damian Asam** 1686–1739, and **Egid Quirin Asam** 1692–1750
   Bavaria 1714–41; Baroque

5 **(Johann) Bathalsar Neumann** 1687–1753
   Germany 1718–52; Rococo

6 **Johann Michael Fischer** 1692–1766
   South Germany c1727–66; Rococo

7 **Richard Boyle, 3rd Earl of Burlington** 1694–1753
   England 1717–32; Palladian

8 **Ange-Jacques Gabriel** 1698–1782
   France 1728–68; Neoclassical

Note: Data under the architect's name and life dates gives the successive
sites of his work, the dates of his working life (to death or completion of
last-known building or treatise), and the style(s) he worked in.

ARCHITECTS' LIFELINES 1700–1990

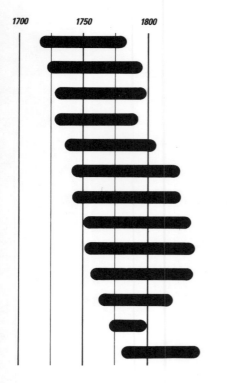

1700   *1750*   *1800*

1700–1800

1   **Lancelot (Capability) Brown** 1716–83
England, Ireland 1740–78; Palladian

2   **Sir William Chambers** 1723–96
Britain, Ireland 1755–86; Palladian/Neoclassical

3   **Étienne-Louis Boulée** 1728–99
France 1762–99; Neoclassical

4   **Robert Adam** 1728–92
Britain, Ireland 1750–92; Neoclassical

5   **Claude-Nicholas Ledoux** 1736–1806
France 1766–92; Neoclassical

6   **George Dance the Younger** 1741–1825
England, Ireland 1761–1813; Neoclassical/Gothic Revival

7   **Thomas Jefferson** 1743–1826
Virginia, Washington DC 1769–1826; Jeffersonian/Neoclassical

8   **John Nash** 1752–1835
England, Wales, Ireland 1778–1832; Neoclassical/Gothic Revival/Regency

9   **Sir John Soane** 1753–1837
England, Ireland c1780–1828; Neoclassical

10   **Thomas Telford** 1757–1834
Britain, Sweden 1780–1831; Neoclassical/Industrial

11   **Benjamin Henry Latrobe** 1764–1820
England, USA pre-1796–1820; Greek and Gothic Revival

12   **Friedrich Gilly** 1772–1800
Prussia 1794–1800; Gothic Revival/Neoclassical

13   **Karl Friedrich Schinkel** 1781–1841
Prussia 1810–38; Neoclassical/Gothic Revival/Romanesque

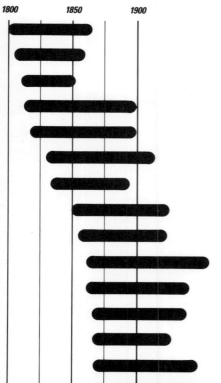

1800   *1850*   *1900*

1800–1870

1   **Sir Joseph Paxton** 1801–65
England, France, Ireland, New York 1836–65; Victorian engineering

2   **Isambard Kingdom Brunel** 1806–59
England, Wales, Ireland, Italy 1825–59; Victorian engineering

3   **Augustus Welby Pugin** 1812–52
England, Ireland, France 1836–51; Gothic Revival

4   **William Butterfield** 1814–1900
England 1844–92; Gothic Revival

5   **John Ruskin** 1819–1900
England 1849–53; Gothic Revival

6   **Philip Speakman Webb** 1831–1915
England 1859–1901; Arts and Crafts

7   **William Morris** 1834–96
England 1856–96; Arts and Crafts

8   **Antoni y Cornet Gaudi** 1852–1926
Barcelona 1878–1926; Art Nouveau

9   **Louis Henry Sullivan** 1856–1924
USA 1873–1924; Chicago School

10   **Henri van de Velde** 1863–1957
Belgium, Paris, Germany, Holland 1895–1954; Art Nouveau

11   **Charles Robert Ashbee** 1863–1942
England 1887–1911; Arts and Crafts

12   **Peter Behrens** 1868–1940
Germany, St Petersburg, Austria, Northampton 1899–1936; Art Nouveau

13   **Charles Rennie Mackintosh** 1868–1928
Scotland, Northampton 1889–1914; Art Nouveau

14   **Tony Garnier** 1869–1948
Lyons, Boulogne-Brillancourt 1898–1935; International Modern

15   **Frank Lloyd Wright** 1869–1959
USA, Tokyo 1893–1956; 'Prairie School'/International Modern

©DIAGRAM

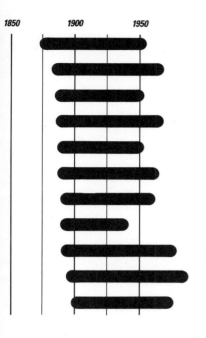

1870–1900

1 **Auguste Perret** 1874–1954
France, Casablanca 1903–50; Art Nouveau/Neoclassical/International Modern

2 **Walter Gropius** 1883–1969
Europe, USA 1906–69; International Modern/Bauhaus/Expressionist

3 **Vladimir Tatlin** 1885–1953
Russia 1913–22; Constructivist

4 **Ludwig Mies van der Rohe** 1886–1969
Europe, USA 1901–69; Expressionist/Bauhaus/International Modern

5 **Erich Mendelssohn** 1887–1953
Germany, England, Palestine, USA 1912–53; Expressionist/International Modern

6 **Le Corbusier** 1887–1965
Switzerland, France, Rio, New York, Harvard, India, Germany, Tokyo 1912–64

7 **Jacobus Johannes Pieter Oud** 1890–1963
Holland 1916–63; De Stijl/'Beton-Rococo'

8 **Eleazar Markevich Lissitsky** 1890–1941
Russia, Germany 1919–30s; Constructivist

9 **Pier Luigi Nervi** 1891–1979
Italy, Paris, Caracas, Montreal, Sydney, USA 1913–79; Modern

10 **Ove Arup** 1895–1988
England, Sydney, 1930– ; International Modern

11 **Hugo Alvar Henrik Aalto** 1898–1976
Finland, USA, Baghdad, Germany, Bologna, Iran 1921–72; Modern

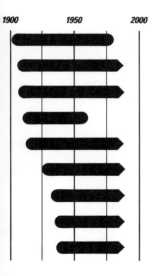

1900–1990

1 **Marcel Lajos Breuer** 1902–81
Germany, Switzerland, England, USA, France, Rotterdam 1928–68; Modern

2 **Philip Cortelyou Johnson** b1906
USA 1932– ; International Modern/ Post Modern

3 **Oscar Niemeyer** b1907
Brazil, New York, Berlin, France 1934– ; International Modern

4 **Eero Saarinen** 1910–61
USA, Oslo, London 1936–61; International Modern

5 **Kenzo Tange** b1913
Japan, Nigeria, 1946– ; International Modern

6 **James Stirling** b1926
Britain, Germany, USA 1950– ; Modern/Brutalism/Post Modern

7 **Richard Rogers** b1933
Britain, France, Princeton NJ, 1963– ; Modern/High Tech

8 **Sir Norman Foster** b1935
England, Hong Kong 1963– ; High Tech

9 **Quinlan Terry** b1937
England 1960s– ; Neoclassical

MAJOR ARCHITECTURAL SITES
GREEK AND ROMAN

HADRIAN'S WALL

•YORK

•CHESTER
•WROXETER

CAERLEON
BATH•
VERULAMIUM
•LONDON
SILCHESTER

RHEIMS•   TRIER•

•AUTUN

•PERIGUEUX

VERONA•   •POLA

•ORANGE   RIMINI
NIMES• •ST REMY   ANCONA   SPLIT
ARLES   FIESOLE•
•SEGOVIA   PERUGIA•
TARRAGONA•   •TIVOLI
•ALCANTARA   HERCULANEUM
•POMPEII
•PAESTUM

ROME
OSTIA
VEII   •LOCR
TAUROMEN
CHERCHEL   DJEMILA•   CARTHAGE•   •SYRACUSE
DOUGGA•
TIMGAD•   PIAZZA ARMERI
•TEBESSA   AGRIGENTUM
EL DJEM•   SELINUS
SEGESTA

SABRATHA•
LEPTIS MAGNA

0   500 miles

0   800 km

Note: Predominantly Greek or Hellenistic sites are in italic type.

©DIAGRAM

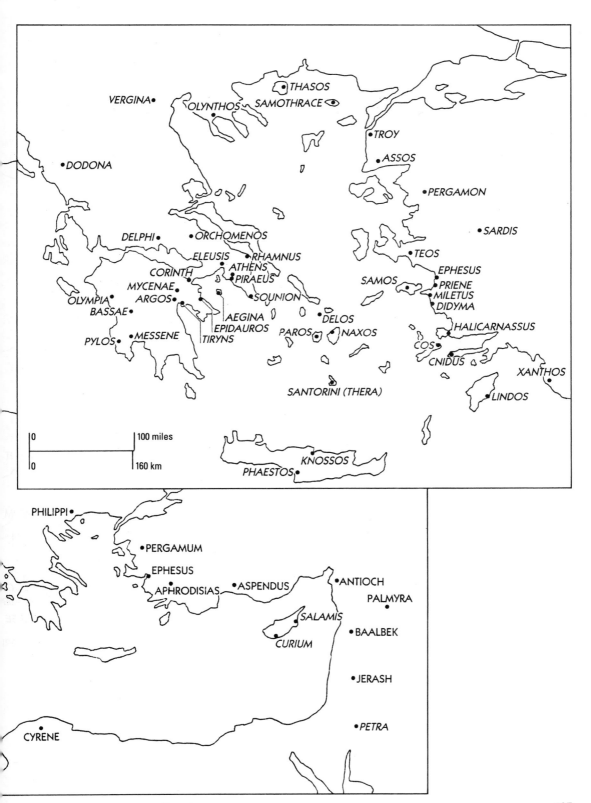

VERGINA•

•DODONA

OLYNTHOS•

•THASOS

SAMOTHRACE

•TROY

•ASSOS

•PERGAMON

•SARDIS

DELPHI•

•ORCHOMENOS

ELEUSIS•

•RHAMNUS

CORINTH

ATHENS

•PIRAEUS

MYCENAE•

•TEOS

•EPHESUS

SAMOS

•PRIENE

•MILETUS

•DIDYMA

OLYMPIA•

ARGOS•

BASSAE•

•SOUNION

AEGINA

EPIDAUROS

TIRYNS

•DELOS

PAROS•

NAXOS

HALICARNASSUS

COS

PYLOS•

•MESSENE

CNIDUS

XANTHOS•

SANTORINI (THERA)

•LINDOS

| 0 | | 100 miles |
| 0 | | 160 km |

KNOSSOS•

PHAESTOS•

PHILIPPI•

•PERGAMUM

EPHESUS•

APHRODISIAS•

•ASPENDUS

•ANTIOCH

PALMYRA

SALAMIS

CURIUM

•BAALBEK

•JERASH

•PETRA

CYRENE•

©DIAGRAM

- DURHAM
- FOUNTAINS ABBEY
- LUBECK
- CLONFERT (Ireland)
- PETERBOROUGH
- HEREFORD
- NORWICH
- BRANDENBURG
- TEWKESBURY
- ELY
- HILDESHEIM
- GLOUCESTER
- GERNRODE
- OXFORD
- ST ALBANS
- LONDON
- EXETER
- WINCHESTER
- CANTERBURY
- CHICHESTER
- TOURNAI
- COLOGNE
- AIX-LA-CHAPELLE
- MARIA LAACH
- LAACH
- LIMBURG
- ASCHAFFENBURG
- TRIER
- MAINZ
- BAMBERG
- BAYEUX
- LESSAY
- BERNIÊRS-SUR-MER
- WORMS
- CAEN
- SERQUIGNY
- SPEYER
- ST DENIS
- MONT ST MICHEL
- VERNEUIL
- PARIS
- STRASBOURG
- REGENSBURG
- CHATEAUDUN
- ORLEANS
- MUNICH
- ANGERS
- TOURS
- FONTEVRAULT
- SELLES S CHER
- VEZELAY
- DIJON
- BASEL
- ST AIGNAN-SUR-CHER
- LA CHARITE
- ST GALL
- AUTUN
- CITEAUX
- POITIERS
- FONTGOMBAULT
- TOURNUS
- CLUNY
- ECHILLAIS
- AULNAY
- CLERMONT FERRAND
- COMO
- BERGAMO
- ANGOULEME
- ISSOIRE
- VIENNE
- MONZA
- MILAN
- VERONA
- PERIGUEUX
- GDE CHARTREUSE
- PAVIA
- CREMONA
- VENICE
- CAHORS
- ASTI
- PIACENZA
- PARMA
- GENOA
- BOLOGNA
- RAVENNA
- AVIGNON
- CARRARA
- PISTOIA
- TOULOUSE
- ST GILLES
- ARLES
- VENCE
- LUCCA
- FIESOLE
- SANTIAGO
- AIX
- PISA
- FLORENCE
- CARCASSONNE
- ASSISI
- RIPOLL
- TOSCANELLA
- MONTE S ANGELO
- TRANI
- BARI
- BITONTO
- TARRAGONA

0   100 miles

0   160 km

PALERMO
MONREALE
CEFALU

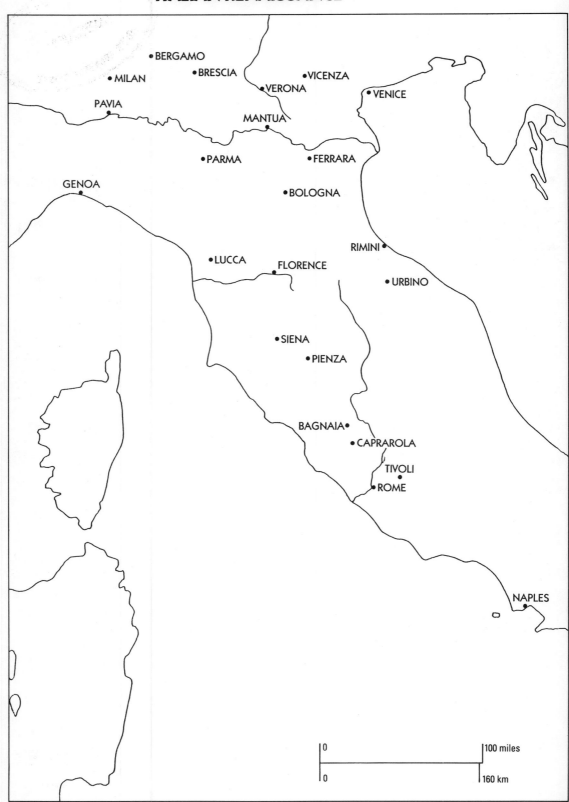

BERGAMO

MILAN

BRESCIA

VICENZA

VERONA

VENICE

PAVIA

MANTUA

PARMA

FERRARA

BOLOGNA

GENOA

RIMINI

LUCCA

FLORENCE

URBINO

SIENA

PIENZA

BAGNAIA

CAPRAROLA

TIVOLI

ROME

NAPLES

| 0 | | 100 miles |
| 0 | | 160 km |

©DIAGRAM

MAJOR ARCHITECTURAL SITES
EUROPEAN RENAISSANCE

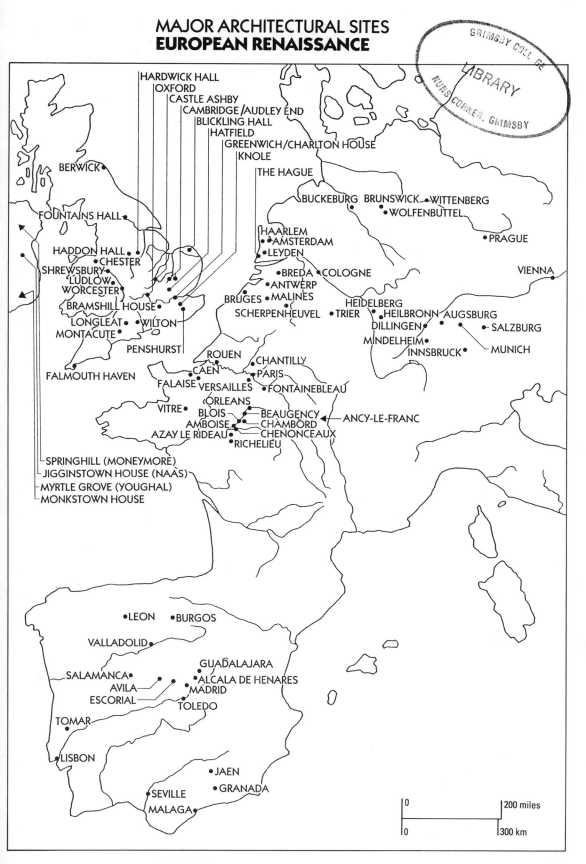

HARDWICK HALL
OXFORD
CASTLE ASHBY
CAMBRIDGE /AUDLEY END
BLICKLING HALL
HATFIELD
GREENWICH/CHARLTON HOUSE
KNOLE
THE HAGUE

BERWICK

FOUNTAINS HALL

HADDON HALL
CHESTER
SHREWSBURY
LUDLOW
WORCESTER
BRAMSHILL HOUSE
LONGLEAT • WILTON
MONTACUTE
PENSHURST

FALMOUTH HAVEN

SPRINGHILL (MONEYMORE)
JIGGINSTOWN HOUSE (NAAS)
MYRTLE GROVE (YOUGHAL)
MONKSTOWN HOUSE

BUCKEBURG BRUNSWICK • WITTENBERG
WOLFENBUTTEL
PRAGUE

HAARLEM
AMSTERDAM
LEYDEN

BREDA COLOGNE
ANTWERP
BRUGES • MALINES
SCHERPENHEUVEL • TRIER

HEIDELBERG
HEILBRONN AUGSBURG
DILLINGEN
MINDELHEIM
INNSBRUCK

VIENNA

SALZBURG
MUNICH

ROUEN
CAEN
FALAISE
VITRE
ORLEANS
BLOIS
AMBOISE
AZAY LE RIDEAU
RICHELIEU

CHANTILLY
PARIS
VERSAILLES • FONTAINEBLEAU

BEAUGENCY
CHAMBORD
CHENONCEAUX

ANCY-LE-FRANC

LEON • BURGOS
VALLADOLID
GUADALAJARA
SALAMANCA • ALCALA DE HENARES
AVILA
ESCORIAL
MADRID
TOLEDO
TOMAR
LISBON
JAEN
GRANADA
SEVILLE
MALAGA

| 0 | 200 miles |
| 0 | 300 km |

©DIAGRAM